Twice as Deadly Volume One

16 Deadly Serial Killer Teams and Couples

Robert Keller

D1416498

Please Leave Your Review of This Book At
http://bit.ly/kellerbooks

ISBN-13: 978-1542647434

ISBN-10: 1542647436

© 2017 by Robert Keller

robertkellerauthor.com

Table of Contents

Douglas Clark & Carol Bundy

At around midday on Thursday, June 12, 1980, a Caltrans employee was cleaning up trash along the Ventura Freeway when he came across a nude body, lying face down among the brush on an embankment. The man staggered back, then started hurriedly down the slope to alert his supervisor. He'd taken only a few steps when he spotted a second corpse, this one fully clothed but with eyes staring blankly skyward. A bullet hole perforated the girl's forehead and there was fresh blood on her face which seemed to indicate that she had not been there long.

When Investigators arrived on the scene, they quickly confirmed that assessment. It looked like the two teenaged girls had been killed elsewhere, then dumped on the steeply sloping embankment. Neither of the victims was carrying ID and detectives assumed that they'd been hitchhikers or runaways. Either way, they'd accepted the wrong ride.

The bodies went to the morgue while detectives began working the police department's missing persons reports, hoping to find a clue to the victims' identity. As it turned out, a couple of teenagers, of similar description, had been reported missing. The next day – Friday the 13th – Angelo Marano of Huntington Beach, California arrived to view the bodies. Within minutes, his worst fears were confirmed. The dead girls were his 15-year-old daughter, Gina, and his stepdaughter, Cynthia Chandler, aged 16. He and his wife had spent a frantic couple of days searching for them.

Autopsies were conducted and indicated that the girls had been dead for approximately twelve hours when they'd been found. Each had been shot with a small caliber pistol - Gina, twice in the head, Cynthia in the head and chest. One of the girls had been sodomized, and there were indications that the bodies had been "sexually tampered with," most likely after death.

Evidence in the case was scant, and the police were far from confident of catching the perpetrator. Then, on Saturday, June 14, a detective at the Van Nuys PD fielded a call from a distraught woman, who claimed to know the identity of the killer. He was her lover, she said, and the two teenagers were not his first victims. Pressed for details, the caller hung up, leaving the detective convinced that the call was a hoax. It wasn't.

Eleven days later, on June 23, two more bodies turned up, shot in similar fashion. The first was Karen Jones, a 24-year-old prostitute. She'd been shot in the head with a small-caliber weapon and dumped behind the Burbank studios. The second was a somewhat more gruesome find.

At around 7:15 a.m., the headless body of a woman was discovered behind the Sizzler restaurant in Studio City. The victim was identified as Exxie Wilson, a 20-year-old prostitute who'd recently moved to L.A. from Little Rock, Arkansas. She was a friend of Karen Jones, the murder victim found earlier. A search of the area failed to turn up the missing head, and there were no clues as to the identity of the killer, either. The police, however, were convinced that the perpetrator was the same man who'd killed Gina Marano and Cynthia Chandler.

In the early hours of June 27, a man named Jonathan Caravello was parking his car in the alley behind his apartment building, when he struck something lying on the ground. As he got out of the vehicle, he spotted an ornate wooden box. Thinking that he might have found something valuable, he lifted the object and unlatched the clasp. The box felt weighty and had an odd smell to it. Caravello flipped the lid and shifted aside the layer of crushed velvet that lined the top. Then he let out a gasp and dropped his find. It contained a human head. Caravello ran for his apartment to call the police.

The head was soon identified as that of Exxie Wilson, and there was evidence that it had been stored in a freezer and recently washed. The medical examiner removed a .25 caliber bullet from the skull, which was matched to the weapon that had killed Karen Jones, Gina Marano, and Cynthia Chandler. Less than a year after the capture of the notorious "Hillside Stranglers" it appeared that L.A. had another serial killer on the loose.

And a fifth victim was soon added to the body count. On June 30, a group of friends walking a ravine in the San Fernando Valley, found the mummified remains of a woman. She was between 17 and 25, about 5'7" with reddish-blond hair. She been shot three times with a small caliber pistol and had been out in the open for approximately three weeks. That would make her the first in the series if ballistics linked her to the other four murder victims. It did. She'd been killed with the same weapon.

An identification of the victim came soon after. She was seventeen-year-old Marnette Comer, a prostitute who had last been seen alive on June 1. Unfortunately for Marnette, she'd gotten into a car with the wrong person.

Serial killers usually target a specific kind of victim – male or female; black or white; straight or gay – so the next murder was not initially linked to the Sunset Strip Slayer, as the press was now calling him.

Jack Murray was a building superintendent and sometime country singer who performed at a local tavern called Little Nashville. On August 9, police were called to Murray's van, which had been left standing unattended at the curb for five days. People were complaining about the foul smell emanating from the vehicle. Inside, a gruesome find awaited officers. Murray's body was headless and, after nearly a week locked in the van, in the midst of a heat wave, it was blistered, blackened, and badly decomposed. Still, police were able to tell that he'd been stabbed several times and that chunks of flesh had been hacked from his buttocks.

Aside from the beheading, and shell casings found at the scene, there was nothing to suggest any connection to the Sunset Strip murders. But there was a link, and this would be provided on August 11 when a manager at the Valley Medical Center in Van Nuys called the police. One of their employees, she said, had just confessed to murder.

Police rushed to the scene and were told that Carol Bundy, an overweight, 37-year-old nurse, had broken down and admitted to them that she and a man named Douglas Clark had carried out the Sunset Strip slayings. However, Bundy had fled the premises before police could get there.

Units were dispatched to Bundy's home, where she was placed under arrest. She handed over to the officers three pairs of panties which she said came from the victims, as well as a photo album of her lover, Douglas Clark, engaged in sexual acts with an 11-year-old girl. And she had one more shocking revelation to share. Clark hadn't killed Jack Murray, she said. She'd done that one herself.

Another team had already gone to Clark's place of work and arrested him for sexual offenses with a minor as well as being an accomplice in the Jack Murray murder. But investigators were far more interested in the other information Carol Bundy had shared with them. If Bundy was telling the truth, Douglas Clark was the Sunset Strip Slayer.

Carol Bundy had endured a hard life, brutalized and humiliated by an abusive mother, then forced into an incestuous relationship with her father after her mother's death. An overweight and frumpy girl, she became promiscuous early in life, realizing that it was a way to get attention from boys. At 17, she escaped her father's attentions by marrying a 56-year-old man. By 36, when she arrived in Los Angeles, she already had three failed marriages behind her.

Bundy had two young sons, 5 and 9, in tow. She also had a catalog of health problems and wore thick glasses. She was overweight, insecure and desperate for attention. So when Jack Murray, the superintendent of the apartment building she'd just moved into, showed her some kindness, Carol was instantly smitten. She and Murray became lovers.

But Murray was married, and when Carol's attentions towards him began to become obsessive, he dumped her. Carol responded by stalking Jack and then trying to bribe his wife into leaving him and eventually threatening her. She also took to spending every evening at the Little Nashville country music bar, where Jack worked as a singer.

Jack continued to ignore her, but just after Christmas in 1979, Carol managed to attract the eye of another man sitting at the bar. Douglas Clark was blond, good-looking and sophisticated. He was charming and well-spoken and enjoyed quoting from literature and peppering his speech with French phrases. He was also an arch-predator who knew that unattractive, overweight women were easy prey. A few kind words and they were putty in his hands, providing him with money, free housing, and whatever else he needed. Carol Bundy certainly fell into this category. Soon after they met, they became lovers, and Clark moved into her apartment.

Carol could hardly believe her luck. Her new beau was not only handsome and exciting, but he was a sensitive and understanding lover too. By the time he started sharing with her his disturbing fantasies about torture, necrophilia, and murder, she was not so much repulsed as intrigued. When he asked her to purchase two .25-caliber Raven automatics and register them in her name, she did so without question. Such was her devotion to Clark that she even agreed to bring other women into their relationship for threesomes, including an eleven-year-old girl who lived across the hall. "It was a gift," she'd later say, "to please him."

But it seemed that the more Carol did for Doug, the less he cared for her. He became demanding and controlling, threatening frequently to leave. He stopped sleeping with her, preferring instead to bring prostitutes home. And he began talking about committing a murder, although Carol didn't take any of that seriously. She didn't think he had it in him.

Then, one day in April 1980, Doug went out in Carol's Buick station wagon and came home covered in blood. He told her that he'd been with a girl in the car when her boyfriend had attacked him. Carol didn't question his story. A week later, he again arrived with blood on his clothes. This time, he said he'd hunted the boyfriend down and killed him. Again, Carol didn't bother challenging his account. Douglas, she knew, was prone to flights of fantasy. But the next day, she'd have reason to reassess that judgment, when she found a bag in her car that contained blood-stained women's clothing. Pressed for an explanation, Doug admitted that he'd picked up two teenaged girls (Gina Marano and Cynthia Chandler) and killed them.

Clark said that he'd spotted the girls waiting at a bus stop on Sunset Strip and had tried to talk one of them (Cynthia) into the car. But the girl wouldn't go without her friend. Once they were in the car, be drove to a deserted car park where he produced a gun and forced Cynthia to perform oral sex on him. While she was doing that, he shot her in the head. Gina tried to jump out of the vehicle but Clark shot her before she could get away. He then pumped another bullet into each of the girls, shooting Gina in the head and Cynthia in the heart.

With the two girls now lying dead on the floor of the car, Clark drove to a garage he rented in Burbank. There he laid both the corpses out on an old mattress and "played with them." Finally, he pushed his penis into Cynthia's mouth and vagina and sodomized Gina. He later dumped their bodies at the side of the highway.

It was a quite horrific story, and yet Bundy found herself intrigued and even a little bit aroused by it. She made Clark promise that he'd take her along the next time. Clark said that he would.

(Carol Bundy must have had second thoughts about this, because she called the Van Nuys PD just a few days later on June 14.)

Less than a week later, on June 20, Clark informed Bundy that he was going out to look for another victim. By now, she was apparently over her confessional phase. In fact, she agreed with Clark beforehand that it would be her who did the killing.

In Hollywood, Clark lured a young prostitute named Cathy into the car and negotiated a deal. Cathy agreed to perform oral sex on Clark while Bundy watched from the back seat. The plan was that Bundy would indicate to Clark when she wanted to shoot the hooker. But before she'd had the chance to do that, Clark drew his gun and shot Cathy in the head. The sight of the woman being killed, the smell of blood and cordite, excited her, Bundy would later admit.

After cleaning up the blood in the car, Clark and Bundy drove to the Hollywood Freeway and dumped Cathy's body near the Magic Mountain amusement park. But Clark was still not satisfied. After dropping Bundy off at the apartment, he returned to the Sunset Strip alone. There, he picked up Exxie Wilson and drove her to the lot next to the Sizzler restaurant in Studio City. He paid for oral sex. While Wilson was carrying out the act on him, he shot her in the head.

Clark didn't bother looking for a place to dump the body this time. He left it in the lot behind the restaurant. Before he did, however, he fetched his pre-prepared "murder kit" from the trunk, and used one of the knives it contained to remove Exxie Wilson's head. This he carried away with him in a black garbage bag.

But Clark was just leaving the parking lot when a thought struck him. Exxie had been with another woman when he'd picked her up. That woman could likely identify him, which meant that she had to die. Karen Jones wasn't difficult to find or to talk into the car. Clark shot her in the head, then pushed her from the vehicle near Burbank studios.

Back at Bundy's apartment, Clark placed Exxie Wilson's head in the freezer. Over the next few days, he'd regularly take it out and use it as a necrophilic oral sex toy. Carol would also have her fun with the macabre keepsake. She'd apply makeup and style the hair. "It was like a big Barbie doll," she'd later tell detectives. Wilson's head was later dumped in the alleyway, where it would be discovered by Jonathan Caravello.

Douglas Clark had by now murdered six young women, and there is every indication that he'd have gone on to kill many more. But his partner in crime was slowly unraveling. For all her devotion to Doug, Carol was still obsessed with Jack Murray and determined to win back his affections. Her way of going about this was to drop hints about the Sunset Strip Slayings and then to come right out and admit that Doug Clark was the killer and she his accomplice. Murray, unsurprisingly, did not believe her. But on August 3, Carol showed him one of the "murder kits" that she had prepared for Doug, containing knives, restraints, gloves, plastic bags and cleaning materials. Now, at last, Jack believed her. But his response wasn't what she'd intended. He told her that she should turn Doug in to the police and hinted that he might call in an anonymous tip-off himself. That was when Carol decided that Jack would have to die.

Jack Murray was lured back to his van at 2:30 that same day, under the pretext of a sexual liaison with Carol. Once inside, she got him to lie on his stomach and then shot him twice in the back of the head. Then she stabbed him half a dozen times in the back and flayed at his buttocks. Realizing the police could probably match the bullets by ballistics, she cut off Jack's head, dropped it into a plastic bag and took it home with her. Later, she and Clark got rid of it.

The stench of decomposition had eventually led to the discovery of Jack Murray's body, but before the investigation even got under way, Carol Bundy had had her meltdown and confessed. By August 11, both she and Doug Clark were in custody.

Douglas Clark went on trial in October 1982, accused of six murders. He entered not guilty pleas to all of the charges and insisted that Bundy and Jack Murray were the perpetrators. Acting as his own attorney, he quickly alienated the judge and jury with his arrogance, insults, and outbursts. No one was spared his caustic tongue, not even the attorneys appointed to assist with his defense.

On January 28, 1983, after five days of deliberation, the jury returned a guilty verdict on all six counts of first-degree murder. Clark urged the court to sentence him to death, and it was happy to oblige, passing judgment on March 16, 1983. Clark was then transported to San Quentin's death row. He's still there, over three decades later.

At Carol Bundy's trial, she entered guilty pleas to two charges of first-degree murder and was sentenced to consecutive terms of 25 years to life. She died of heart failure at the California Institution for Women on December 9, 2003. She was 61 years old.

John Duffy & David Mulcahy

The science of criminal profiling is an important investigative tool these days, a cornerstone of any serial homicide investigation. However, there was a time when such techniques were ridiculed by law enforcement officers, considered about as useful as phrenology or palm reading. The case that changed all that was the pursuit of the so-called, 'Railway Killer,' a brutal serial killer who raped and murdered three women in London during the mid-1980's.

The murders were, in fact, the culmination of a protracted crime spree. Beginning in 1982, a series of violent rapes had been committed in and around train stations across London, Surrey, and the Home Counties. The perpetrators were two masked men, working together. Over a period of 12 months, 18 women would fall prey to this sinister pair, described by their victims as working with an almost telepathic understanding of each other.

Then, in 1983, the attacks mysteriously ceased, only to resume again in 1984. This time though, the perpetrator was a sole rapist, and his attacks were far more frequent, culminating in 1985 with three rapes in a single night.

Something clearly had to be done to stop this criminal, and the police responded by launching Operation Hart, one of Britain's biggest criminal investigations ever. Yet, despite the breadth of this undertaking, the police had very little to go on. They had figured out by now that the rapist had an in-depth knowledge of the rail system, and they knew that the man they sought was small in stature. Other than that, the only description they had was of the criminal's eyes, said to be, "cold blue, staring, almost like lasers."

They knew also that he carried a knife and must have feared that, unless they caught him soon, someone was going to get seriously hurt.

On the cold afternoon of December 29, 1985, 19-year-old Alison Day left her home in Hornchurch, Essex and boarded a bus for Hackney Wick railway station. Her fiancé, Paul Tidiman, was working overtime that day, and the pair had agreed to meet up at the printing works where Paul was employed. This was just a short walk from the station, but to reach it, Alison had to traverse a darkened path that ran alongside a canal. It was on that path that she met her killer.

When Alison didn't show, Paul became anxious. Eventually, he left work and walked to the nearby station where he stood on the platform, calling her name. Little did he know that she lay just 100 yards away, raped and murdered.

A massive search was launched but turned up nothing until January 15, 1986, when Allison was found floating, face down in the River Lee. Her blouse had been cut into three strips, two of which had been used to gag and bind her. The third piece was around her neck, where it had been used as a tourniquet. The killer had placed stones in the pockets of her sheepskin coat in an effort to sink the body and destroy evidence. And he'd succeeded, in part at least. Two weeks in the water had failed to obliterate the fibers that still clung stubbornly to the fabric of the coat. These were collected and held for later comparison, should a suspect be arrested.

Given the proximity of the murder to a rail station, the officers working the Alison Day inquiry were convinced that there was a connection to the 'Railway Rapist' case. Operation Hart detectives were less enthused by the idea and declined to lend their resources to the murder inquiry. It was a tragic mistake.

Maartje Tamboezer was just 15-years-old, one of 3 sisters, the daughter of a Dutch businessman living in West Horsley, Surrey. On the afternoon of Thursday, April 17, 1986, Maartje was excited about her upcoming holiday. She wanted to buy some candy to take with her on the trip and in late afternoon, she decided to cycle to the nearby village of East Horsley. When she hadn't returned by early evening, her frantic parents called the Surrey Police.

The next morning, two men walking along a path that ran adjacent to the A246, between Guildford and Leatherhead, came across Maartje's body. She was bound by the wrists and had been savagely beaten. The tourniquet that had strangled her was still around her neck and the killer had tried to set fire to her corpse, presumably in an effort to obliterate forensic evidence. The victim's bicycle was found nearby, propped against a tree.

The police also came across an interesting clue, a length of bright orange rope stretched across the footpath at chest height. This had obviously been set there to force a cyclist coming up the path to stop and dismount. Detectives surmised that Maartje had then been dragged into nearby woods, raped, beaten, and finally garroted. Aside from the rope, police found an unusually small footprint at the scene. And the postmortem yielded another clue. One of the victim's neck bones was broken. The pathologist believed that the injury had been caused by a 'karate chop.'

As Surrey police continued their inquiries, they got their most promising lead yet. Passengers traveling on the 6:07 p.m. train from Horsley to London, on the day of the murder, reported a man rushing onto the platform as the train was departing, and trying to force his way onboard, resulting in the guard having to reopen the self-closing doors. The man was small in stature, and more than one passenger described him as having piercing blue eyes. The police wondered whether this might be the man who had left the footprint. They checked thousands of discarded train tickets for fingerprints but came up empty.

There were, however, additional clues from the crime scene. Semen lifted from the victim gave the killer's blood type as group A. Then there was the string used to bind the girl's hands. It was a brand called Somyarn, and was unusual in that it was made from paper, not the usual hessian or plastic.

The police were still following up on these leads when the Railway Killer struck again. The victim was a 29-year-old secretary named Anne Lock. Anne had recently married and had only just returned from her honeymoon in the Seychelles. On the night of Sunday, May 18, she worked late at her job at London Weekend Television. After finishing her shift, she took a train to Brookman's Park near Potter's Bar, Hertfordshire, arriving there at around 10 p.m. Alighting the train, she walked quickly towards the bicycle shed where she had left her bike. She was never seen alive again.

The disappearance of Anne Lock was soon linked to the murders of Alison Day and Maartje Tamboezer and resulted in Surrey and Hertfordshire police working together to launch the biggest manhunt undertaken in Britain since the Yorkshire Ripper inquiry of the 1970's. Information on the murders was also fed into the Operation Hart database, enabling detectives to narrow their initial list of over 5000 suspects down to 1,999. Number 1,594 was John Duffy, a slightly built Irishman, who worked as a carpenter for British Rail.

Duffy had earned himself a place on the suspect list due to a charge that he'd raped his (then estranged, now ex) wife in August 1985. Then, on Saturday, May 17, 1986, he was arrested for loitering at North Weald Railway station and found to be in possession of a butterfly knife. Duffy said that the knife was for use in his martial arts class, and without evidence of any offense, the police had no option but to release him. However, details of his arrest were logged with the police and on July 17, he was brought in for questioning.

Duffy arrived with a solicitor in tow and refused to give a blood sample, immediately arousing suspicion. Detectives also couldn't help but notice that he fit the description of the man they sought, small in stature, with pockmarked skin, and those piercing blue eyes that several victims had described. His reference to a martial arts class also got detectives thinking about the broken bone in Maartje Tamboezer's neck, and how the pathologist believed a karate blow might have caused it.

Four days later, a maintenance team discovered Anne Lock's body on an overgrown embankment near Brookman's Park Station. Like the other victims she had been garroted, her hands bound with the same coarse string. The killer had also tried to burn her corpse.

Detectives now decided to bring Duffy in for a second round of questioning. To their astonishment, they found that he had been admitted to a psychiatric hospital in North London and that doctors there were refusing access to him. According to Duffy he'd been attacked and beaten by two men and had lost his memory as a result. The police were skeptical about his claims but couldn't disprove them.

Duffy would remain at the hospital for a month, while the police moved on to other suspects. He was at liberty again by the time a 14-year-old Watford schoolgirl was raped on October 21. The girl described her attacker as small, with a pockmarked face and piercing blue eyes. She also said that he had a German Shepherd Dog with him, who he referred to as Bruce.

The description was a close match for Duffy, and he was rapidly elevated to the top of the suspect list and placed under surveillance. The police were by now almost certain that Duffy was their man. Yet they lacked any concrete evidence against him. In order to firm up their case, they turned to an unusual source.

Criminal profiling had already been in use in the United States for a decade, with experts like John Douglas and Robert Ressler at the forefront of the technology. However, it was still in its infancy in Britain, so when the task force decided to develop a profile of the Railway Killer, they turned to David Canter, a professor of Applied Psychology at the University of Surrey.

Canter was an expert in Behavioral Science, but he had never worked with the police before. When asked to develop the profile, he spent two weeks reading through witness statements and forensic reports as well as mapping the sites of each of the attacks. Eventually, he produced his report, presenting the police with 17 points about the character and behavior of the killer. He even predicted where the killer lived.

Professor Canter's profile would prove to be remarkably accurate, with 13 out of his 17 indicators matching the killer, including; his marital status, his age, build, occupation, and interests. When the police fed this information into the database and compared it against their suspect list, only one name was returned – John Duffy.

On Sunday, November 23, 1986, senior detectives ordered Duffy's arrest and a search of his home. This turned up a wealth of incriminating evidence, including a ball of Somyarn string and fibers similar to those found on Alison Day's coat. Both would be forensically matched to the victims. The police also discovered that Duffy had a German Shepherd Dog named Bruce, as mentioned by one of his victims.

Duffy's trial was held at London's Old Bailey, 14 months later. Many of his rape victims could not bring themselves to face him in court, but five of them did give evidence. He entered not guilty pleas on all charges but was eventually found guilty on five counts of rape and two of murder. In the case of Anne Lock, the jury returned an acquittal due to lack of evidence. He displayed no emotion as he was handed eight life sentences.

But despite his conviction, Duffy refused to name his accomplice, the man who had committed at least 16 rapes with him and who police now believed was also involved in the murders.

They suspected David Mulcahy, a lifelong friend of Duffy, but lacked the evidence to charge him. Mulcahy was brought in for questioning but hung tough over six grueling days. Then, after a search of his house failed to turn up anything incriminating, Mulcahy called a news conference and threatened legal action for wrongful arrest. The police were forced to back off.

Ten years passed and, with John Duffy behind bars and stoically maintaining his silence, Mulcahy must have thought he'd gotten away with murder. Then, in August 1996, another rapist began operating on Hampstead Heath, setting off a chain of events that would eventually bring David Mulcahy to justice.

The rapist's name was Ted Biggs, and he would sexually assault six women before a police operation, dubbed Operation Loudwater, eventually snared him. Before that happened, one of the Loudwater team, DC Caroline Murphy, met DC John Haye in a pub. Haye had worked on the Duffy investigation. The two got talking and quickly realized the similarities between the two cases.

The next day, DC Murphy called Whitehouse prison to ascertain that Duffy was still behind bars, and could not be responsible for the crimes she was investigating. During the course of that inquiry, Murphy learned that Duffy had confided the name of his accomplice to another inmate as David Mulcahy.

At the time of Duffy's arrest, DNA profiling was not yet available as a tool to investigators. Now though, the surviving evidence was re-examined and turned up a match to Mulcahy. Police also found a blunder made by the original investigative team, a fingerprint belonging to David Mulcahy on a rope that had been used to bind one of the victims.

Mulcahy was arrested, and with the DNA evidence against him, prosecutors were confident of a conviction. That conviction became a forgone conclusion when John Duffy agreed to testify, revealing details about the murders that had never been heard before.

Duffy and Mulcahy had known each other all their lives. They made an odd pair, the towering, powerfully-build Mulcahy and the diminutive, pockmarked Duffy. Yet they had been almost inseparable, drawn to each other by a shared love of martial arts and a mutual appetite for cruelty. As youngsters they got their kicks scaring homosexuals on Hampstead Heath and indulging in acts of animal cruelty.

Then, in 1976 they were convicted of causing actual bodily harm after they shot four victims with an air rifle. Shortly afterwards, Mulcahy suggested for the first time that they should rape a woman.

It is easy to see how such an idea would have appeal to the monstrous pair. Each man was plagued by deep feelings of sexual inadequacy - Duffy due to a low sperm count which prevented him from fathering children; Mulcahy because he had difficulty maintaining an erection during normal sex.

According to Duffy, their first victim was meant to be a woman from Hendon, north London, who Mulcahy wanted to 'teach a lesson.' They broke into the her house but left when she failed to come home. Another planned rape was foiled when the intended victim returned home with a male friend.

In 1981, the pair found themselves in court on a theft charge, but escaped with suspended sentences. A year later, they launched the horrific series of rapes that would culminate in murder.

Duffy and Mulcahy became quite accomplished at their craft. They'd prepare a 'rape kit,' consisting of balaclavas, knives, and tape to gag and blindfold their victims. Then they'd hit the streets, trawling for victims while singing along to the sounds of Michael Jackson's 'Thriller.'

As time went by, Mulcahy began to become more and more sadistic. He'd taunt his victims, threatening to gouge their eyes out or slice off their nipples. Their terror seemed to turn him on. He became more physically violent too. On one occasion, Duffy described having to break off an attack because he feared Mulcahy would kill the 16-year-old victim. A month later, according to Duffy, he stopped another attack because of Mulcahy' rage. It was clear by now that the sexual thrill was not enough for Mulcahy. He wanted more.

Four days after Christmas 1985, they targeted Alison Day, forcing her from a path near Hackney Wick station and dragging her to some snow covered playing fields nearby. After both men had raped Alison, she tried to escape and fell into the freezing water of a feeder canal. Duffy claimed that he pulled her out, but Mulcahy was so excited by the incident that he raped the terrified girl again. Mulcahy then tore off a piece of Alison's blouse, twisted it into a tourniquet and strangled her. Later, he told Duffy: "It is God-like, having the decision over life and death."

On April 17, 1986, the pair laid a trap by tying a length of rope across a bicycle path. When 15-year-old Maartje Tamboezer stopped her bike to go around it, they grabbed her and dragged her into some woods where both men raped her.

Mulcahy then struck the girl with a rock to the side of the head, knocking her unconscious. Then he took Maartje's belt and looped it around her throat, before slotting a stick under the belt to form a garrotte. He allegedly told Duffy: "I did the last one, you do this one." After Maartje was dead, they both left, but Mulcahy returned later and set the body alight, stuffing burning tissues into her vagina to destroy forensic evidence.

Just over a month later, the pair ambushed Anne Lock at Brookman's Park station. According to Duffy's account, he raped Anne first. Then, Mulcahy threw him a bunch of keys and sent him to fetch the car. When he returned, Mulcahy told him: "I've taken care of it. She won't identify us now." Duffy said that Mulcahy was buzzing on the drive home. He kept saying: "Keep your eyes open for another one."

David Mulcahy was eventually convicted of three murders, seven rapes, and five charges of conspiracy to commit rape. He was sentenced to life in prison. Neither he nor Duffy will ever be released.

David Alan Gore & Fred Waterfield

David Alan Gore was born in Vero Beach, Florida in 1951. His cousin, Fred Waterfield, was born in the same area a year later, and the two grew up together, developing a bond that made them as close as brothers. By the time they reached their teens, both boys were tall and powerfully built, with Fred the star of the high school football team. By then, the cousins had already acquired a reputation for trouble. They were both obsessed with girls and were not averse to using forceful "persuasion" to have their way with them. Gore had also been fired from an after school job at a gas station, for drilling a peephole in the women's restroom and spying on unsuspecting female customers.

Fast forward a decade, and the cousins had morphed into stereotypical "rednecks," who spent much of their time drinking beer and hunting. Their enthusiasm for sexual violence hadn't waned either, although they'd always managed to stop short of outright rape and thus were able to stay out of the clutches of the law. Then, in 1976, a conversation over a couple of beers turned to the subject of women. Gore bemoaned the fact that they always played so hard to get and Waterfield agreed, adding that, in his opinion, he and Gore should be entitled to have any woman they wanted. By the end of the evening, they had resolved to do just that, to stalk and rape any attractive woman who caught their eye.

The cousins soon got to work pursuing their project and just as soon realized that their plans were not as easy to carry out in practice as they had been in theory. They'd imagined that the women they targeted would simply give in when confronted by two hulking men. They did not. Several potential victims escaped, as much due to the cousins' ineptitude as to anything else. When they eventually did succeed in carrying out a rape, they were promptly arrested. Unfortunately, the victim was so traumatized by her ordeal that she refused to testify in court and the cousins walked free. Shortly after, Waterfield moved to Orlando and their unholy alliance was broken.

By early 1981, Gore had a job as the caretaker of a citrus grove, and was patrolling the streets at night, as an auxiliary sheriff's deputy. Waterfield was managing an auto shop in Orlando, 100 miles away, although he still visited his cousin regularly. It was during one of these visits that he suggested resuming their "hunts." Gore was happy to go along with the plan, although he added one condition. Their last foray had hardly been a success. Had the victim decided to testify they would almost certainly have ended up in prison. This time, no witness would be left alive.

And so it was that a deal was struck. Waterfield, in fact, was so enthused by the plan that he offered Gore a $1,000 bounty for any pretty girl he was able to deliver. Abducting the victims should be easy, he reckoned, since Gore had a Sheriff's badge and could demand compliance. As for the bodies, well there were vast citrus orchards where they could be buried.

On February 19, 1981, Gore spotted 17-year-old Ying Hua Ling embarking from a school bus. He stopped and produced his badge, then demanded to know where Ying Hua lived. Frightened and confused, the girl did not even bother asking what she'd done wrong. She directed Gore to her home, where he also took her mother into custody, handcuffing both women and then marching them to his truck. He then phoned Waterfield in Orlando before driving his victims to the orchard.

Left with some time to kill while he waited for Waterfield, Gore raped both of the women. When Waterfield eventually arrived, he too raped Ying Hua. The cousins then discussed how they would dispose of their victims and decided that Waterfield would strangle Ying Hua, while Gore did the same to her mother. Mrs. Ling, however, was already dead, choked to death by the rope that had been tied around her neck. Waterfield strangled the teenager before departing the scene, leaving Gore to dispose of the bodies. Gore was paid $400, rather than the $1,000 he'd been promised, because Waterfield complained that he'd "asked specifically for a blond."

Five months later, on July 15, Gore was patrolling Round Island Park, when he spotted an attractive blond who he knew his cousin would like. He waited until his target went for a walk on the beach then got to work disabling her car. When the woman, 35-year-old Judith Daley, returned and had trouble starting the vehicle, Gore appeared, flashed his sheriff's badge, and offered to drive Judith to a telephone. Once she was in his truck, however, he produced a gun and then handcuffed her. Then he phoned Waterfield before setting off for the orchard.

Waterfield was delighted with Gore's latest "acquisition." So much so that he paid $1,500 for the pleasure of raping her. Then, after Gore had also had his way with the victim, he strangled her. Judith Daley's disappearance would remain a mystery until two years later, when Gore described her fate to investigators. He said that he'd driven her body to a swamp ten miles west of I-95 and "fed her to the alligators."

A week after the Daley murder, Gore attempted to force a teenager into his pickup but was chased off by the girl's father. The man reported the incident to the police, giving the truck's license plate number. Gore was arrested soon after and although no charges were filed, he was fired from his position as an auxiliary police officer. A couple of weeks later, he was in even deeper trouble when he was caught hiding in the backseat of a woman's car, armed with a pistol and a pair of handcuffs. That offense earned him a 5-year prison term. He served less than two before being paroled. He'd barely hit the streets before he and Waterfield (now living in Vero Beach again) resumed their deadly hunts.

On May 20, 1983, Gore drew a gun on an Orlando prostitute and tried to force her into his vehicle. The woman, however, was able to break free and make a run for it before Gore could snap the cuffs on her. The next victims were not so lucky. Fourteen-year-old runaways Angelica Lavallee and Barbara Byer were hiking along FL-60 when Gore stopped to pick them up. The girls were driven to a remote spot where they were raped by both men before Gore shot them to death. He then dismembered Barbara's body and buried it in a shallow grave. Exhausted by the effort, he simply dumped Angelica's corpse in a nearby canal.

Just over two months later, on July 26, 1983, Vero Beach authorities received a report of a man firing shots at a naked woman on a residential street. Officers rushed to the scene and found a car parked in the driveway of a house. There was blood dripping from the trunk of the vehicle. When an officer popped the lid, he found the naked body of a young woman inside. The victim, later identified as 17-year-old Lynn Elliott, had been shot in the head. The police then entered the house and found David Gore cowering inside. A search of the premises turned up another surprise –14-year-old Regan Martin, naked and tied by her wrists to the rafters in the attic. She was lucky to be alive.

Martin told police that she and Elliott had been hitchhiking when Gore and another man picked them up, threatened them with a gun, and brought them to the house. There they were stripped, tied up and repeatedly raped. Elliott had eventually been able to work her hands free. She'd made a run for it, but Gore had chased after her.

The neighborhood boy who had made the 911 call, filled in the rest of the details. He said that he'd seen the naked girl bolt from the house, chased by a man who was also naked but carrying a gun. The girl might have gotten away, but she stumbled and fell, whereupon the man yanked her to her feet, pushed her up against a tree and shot her twice in the head. He'd then carried her to his car and dumped her in the trunk.

Faced with the eyewitness testimony against him, David Gore broke down and confessed, not just to the murder of Lynn Elliott, but to five more. Convicted of the Elliott murder, he was sentenced to death. Fred Waterfield, his cousin and accomplice, drew two life terms, for the Byer/Levallee murders.

David Gore was executed by lethal injection on April 12, 2012. His final statement was an apology to Lynn Elliot's family: "I want to say to the Elliott family I am sorry for the death of your daughter. I am not the same man I was back then 28 years ago. I hope they can find it in their hearts to forgive me."

To Lynn's father Carl, seated among the witnesses at the execution, those words must have carried a hollow ring.

The Bloody Benders

The story of the Bloody Benders is one of the great, unsolved mysteries of the Old West. It takes place in Kansas shortly after the conclusion of the Civil War. The United States government had recently relocated the Osage Indian tribe from Labette County, Kansas, to make room for new settlers and it was onto these windswept plains that 60-year-old John Bender (known as "Pa") and his son John Jr. rode in late 1870.

They'd soon staked a couple of claims close to the Osage Trail, northeast of the township of Cherryvale. Almost immediately, they set to work, constructing a cabin of 16 by 24 feet, a barn, and a corral. In the meantime, word was sent to their womenfolk, 42-year-old Ma Bender and her daughter Kate, 23 years old at the time of these events.

By the time the women arrived in the fall of 1871, the house and outbuildings had been completed, and Pa and John Jr. had dug a well, started a vegetable garden, and planted the first trees for their intended orchard. The next move was to divide the cabin into two, using wagon canvas. The smaller section of the building served as the Benders' living quarters, the larger was turned into an inn and grocery store.

On the face of it, the Benders made the most unlikely of hoteliers. Pa was of German extraction and spoke no English, his conversation consisting mainly of harsh grunts. Ma wasn't much of a conversationalist either, and was of such a hostile demeanor that her neighbors nicknamed her "She-devil." John Jr. was thought by many to be simple-minded and was prone to idiotic giggling for no reason at all. Which left Kate, the undoubted star in the Bender galaxy. Bubbly and outgoing, she was said by contemporary accounts to be quite beautiful.

But whatever their shortcomings as guesthouse operators, the Benders did have one thing going for them. Their establishment was located just 100 yards south of the Osage Trail and was the only one of its kind for miles in either direction. That made it a convenient stopover for weary travelers. It wasn't long before some of those travelers began coming to harm.

In May 1871, a man named Jones was found in Drum Creek, his skull shattered and his throat cut. In February 1872, the bodies of two men were found, bearing similar injuries. In the winter of that year, a man named George Loncher, and his 18-month-old daughter, disappeared in the region of Osage while on route to Iowa. In spring 1873, a friend of Loncher's, Dr. William York, went looking for him and also vanished.

With stories now rife of bandits picking off travelers along the Osage Trail, Dr. York's brother, Colonel Edward York, launched a search for him. York was well connected (his other brother was Kansas Senator Alexander York), and he put together a search party of 50 men to carry out the mammoth task of questioning every traveler and visiting every homestead along the trail. On March 28, 1873, he arrived at the Bender Inn.

The Benders admitted that Dr. York had spent a night with them but insisted that he had gone on his way the following day. They suggested that he might have run into trouble with the local Indian tribes and while Colonel York conceded that might be a possibility he remained suspicious of the family.

Around the same time, rumors began circulating that the residents of Osage township were behind the disappearances of travelers in the region. Angered by these speculations, town officials called a meeting, which was attended by 75 locals. Both Pa Bender and John Jr. were in attendance and will have listened with interest as the decision was taken to search every homestead between Big Hill Creek and Drum Creek.

Three days later, a neighbor of the Benders was driving his cattle past the Bender Inn when he found their farm animals roaming freely around the premises in an apparently starving condition. On further investigation, he discovered that the inn was empty and the Benders nowhere to be found. He reported the news, but due to poor weather conditions, it would be several days before a search party arrived at the Bender property.

It was quickly apparent that the family had departed in haste. The inn had been left in disarray with all of their personal belongings removed. The search party noticed something else too; a sickening stench pervaded the building. It appeared to be coming from a nailed down trapdoor in the living quarters.

The source of the foul odor was soon apparent. On prying the trapdoor open, the searchers found a small cellar, its floor drenched with clotted blood. A thorough search was then conducted, with the cabin completely lifted from its base and moved aside. Yet, despite these evacuations, no corpses were turned up.

Eventually, after hours of fruitless digging, the search was about to be called off when one of the party noticed a strange subsidence in the earth of the orchard. The diggers then re-directed their efforts and quickly recovered a male body from a shallow grave. It was Dr. William York, the back of his skull caved in by a savage blow, his throat slit from side to side.

Nine more bodies were found the following day, all but one carrying the trademark bludgeoning and knife wounds. The exception was George Loncher's 18-month-old daughter, whose tiny corpse bore no visible signs of trauma. It appeared that she had been buried alive.

Word of the murders spread quickly throughout the region and beyond, with reporters arriving from as far afield as New York and Chicago. Meanwhile, a posse was formed to hunt down the murderous Bender clan and rewards of up to $3,000 were offered for their apprehension.

While those searches were underway, lurid newspaper stories outlined in horrific detail the murderous method of the Benders. It appears that anyone who entered the inn with money or valuables was targeted. The victim would be placed at a table with his back to the canvas wall. Kate Bender would keep him company, regaling him with some or other story. Meanwhile, Pa or John Jr. would creep up behind the canvas wall with a sledgehammer in hand. As soon as the unwary traveler leaned back in his chair, he'd be struck on the head rendering him unconscious. He'd then be dragged into the back room searched and robbed and thrown through the trapdoor, his throat cut for good measure. After dark, the Benders would retrieve the body and bury it. At least 11 victims met their fate in this way.

But where were the Benders? No one knew. Detectives, who had followed their tracks north, had found their wagon with its team of near-starved horses still in harness. But of the family itself, there was not a trace.

The mystery, unfortunately, does not have a definitive outcome. Several posses claimed to have run the family to ground, lynched them and then burned their bodies. Given that there was a $3,000 bounty on their heads (over $50,000 in today's money) this seems unlikely. Surely, anyone who captured the Benders would have brought them back and laid claim to the reward.

What we do know, is that the family fled north to Thayer where they boarded a train. John Jr. and Kate got off at Chanute, then took another train south to Texas. It was rumored that their destination was an outlaw colony in Red River County, an area considered the most lawless region in the United States.

Ma and Pa Bender continued north to Kansas City, from there to St. Louis, Missouri, whereafter they dropped out of sight.

Over the next 50 years, there were many reported sightings of the infamous Benders. In 1884, it was reported that John Bender Sr. had committed suicide in Lake Michigan. And in October 1889, two women suspected of being Ma and Kate Bender were arrested in Niles, Michigan. Despite their protestations that they had been misidentified, they were extradited to Oswego, Kansas to stand trial. Both were later released for lack of evidence.

The mystery of the Bloody Benders endures to this day.

Thierry Paulin & Jean-Thierry Mathurin

Between the years 1984 and 1987, a beast was loose on the streets of Paris. The fiend targeted the most vulnerable victims of all, elderly women who were robbed of their meager possessions then murdered in the most horrendous ways possible, beaten, throttled, asphyxiated, one even forced to drink drain cleaner. At least 18 victims would fall prey to one of the most depraved killers France has ever known, a man named Thierry Paulin, The Monster of Montmartre.

Thierry Paulin entered the world in Fort-de-France, Martinique, on November 28, 1963. His parents were never married, and his father absconded soon after the boy was born. Neither did his mother appear particularly keen on parental responsibility. Thierry was handed over to his paternal grandmother who raised him until the age of 10, when he was reunited with his mother.

But life in his new home was far from ideal. Thierry's mother had by now married, and she had other children. Thierry was made to feel like an outsider and he took out his frustrations on his stepsiblings, beating them frequently and mercilessly. Eventually, his mother decided to call time on the arrangement. She contacted Thierry's biological father and asked if he would take the boy in. The father, who had by now returned to France, agreed, but only because it meant he would no longer have to pay alimony.

Thierry did not settle well in France. As a mixed-race student, he was marginalized by his peers and had few friends. He did poorly at school, flunking out before graduation. At age 17, he volunteered for military service and was accepted into the parachute corps. But even here he was ostracized because of his race. He was also openly homosexual, something that did not sit well with his fellow paratroopers.

Leaving the army in 1984, Paulin returned to his father's apartment in Toulouse. But when he learned that his mother was now living in France, he sought her out, eventually moving into her home in Nanterre, a north Parisian suburb. As it had been in Martinique, though, so it was also in Paris. Paulin's relationship with his mother and her new family quickly deteriorated, and he soon found himself looking for a new place to stay.

At around this time, Paulin began working as a waiter at the "Paradis Latin," a gay bar renowned for its transvestite shows. After a while, he convinced the club owners to let him take to the stage, where he performed a drag act to the tunes of his favorite artist, Eartha Kitt. He soon became a popular performer and attracted the attention of 19-year-old Jean-Thierry Mathurin.

They say that like attracts like and in Mathurin, Thierry Paulin had indeed found a soul mate. Like Paulin, Mathurin had been born and raised in the colonies (in his case, French Guyana) and was the product of a broken home. He was also a drug addict and a petty criminal, known for his cruel streak and quick temper. It wasn't long before he and Paulin became lovers. Soon after, Paris began experiencing a spate of brutal attacks on elderly women.

The first of those attacks occurred on October 5, 1984, when 91-year-old Germaine Petitot was savagely beaten. She survived but was too traumatized to give a description of her assailants. Anna Barbier-Ponthus, 83, wasn't so lucky. She was kicked and punched and then asphyxiated with a pillow. Her killer netted 300 francs (about $50) from the murder.

Over the next two months, eight more elderly women were killed, all of them in and around Paris's 18th precinct. The crimes were marked by extreme overkill. Some of the victims had plastic bags pulled over their heads, others were beaten to a pulp, one had a domestic drain cleaning liquid forced down her throat. The motive in all of these cases appeared to be robbery. However, it was clear that the killers enjoyed inflicting pain and terror on their hapless victims.

Neither were they bothered by conscience. At the time of the murders, Paulin and Mathurin were living an extravagant lifestyle. They spent their nights partying, drinking champagne, and snorting cocaine. And whenever the money ran low, they went trawling again, searching for another elderly victim to rob and brutalize. Then, with the police no closer to solving the case, the murders suddenly stopped. Paulin had left Paris for his father's home in Toulouse, bringing Mathurin with him.

Paulin senior, however, was less than thrilled to see his son. He did not accept Thierry's homosexuality and was certainly not prepared to play host to him and his gay lover. A series of violent fights erupted resulting eventually in Mathurin ending his relationship with Paulin and returning to Paris. Paulin stayed behind in Toulouse a while longer, trying to form a troupe of transvestite artists. When that failed, he moved back to Paris. Soon after his arrival, there was a second wave of murders.

Between December 20, 1985, and June 14, 1986, eight elderly women turned up strangled and beaten to death in their apartments. These murders, however, were different to the former series. The victims had been dispatched quickly, without the torture that had accompanied the earlier killings. The motive, it appeared, was robbery. The police might, in fact, have investigated this as a separate case but for one detail – fingerprint evidence left at the scenes matched those in the earlier murders.

Then, in August 1986, there was another of those unexplained pauses in the series. The reason for the abrupt break would later become clear. Thierry Paulin had attacked a cocaine dealer with a baseball bat and had been sentenced to 16 months in prison. He served a year of that sentence, emerging in the autumn of 1987. He'd barely been released when the murders started up again.

Rachel Cohen, 79, was battered to death on November 25, 1987. That same day, 87-year old Rose Finalteri was found beaten and throttled and barely breathing. Two days later, officers were called to another murder scene. The victim, this time, was 80-year-old Genevieve Germont.

On November 28, 1987, Paulin was partying hard, celebrating his 24th birthday. Unbeknownst to him, Madame Finalteri, the woman he'd strangled, had survived the attack. She'd now regained consciousness and was able to provide a remarkably accurate description of her attacker. She said he was a mixed-race man in his early twenties, with hair like Carl Lewis and an earring in his left ear.

On December 1, a police inspector named Francis Jacob was walking along a street in Montmartre when he spotted a man fitting the description given by Madame Finalteri. Paulin was stopped and questioned, then asked to accompany the inspector to the nearest police station. Two days later, he eventually cracked under interrogation and admitted to 21 murders. Nine of them, the worst ones, the torture murders, had been committed with the assistance of Jean-Thierry Mathurin. Mathurin was taken into custody soon after.

Thierry Paulin would never stand trial for his horrendous crimes.
By early 1988, he was already showing the advanced effects of
AIDS. Within a year he was afflicted with both tuberculosis and
meningitis and was virtually paralyzed. He died in the hospital
wing of Fresnes prison on the night of April 16, 1989.

Left to face the music alone, Jean-Thierry Mathurin tried to put all
of the blame on Paulin, saying that he'd been a mere 'spectator' at
the crime scenes. Given Mathurin's renowned cruelty, this is highly
unlikely. He was convicted of nine murders and sentenced to life in
prison, without the possibility of parole.

Kenneth Bianchi & Angelo Buono

Murders happen every day in a city the size of Los Angeles. And when the victims are prostitutes, they warrant hardly a mention. The lifestyle is dangerous, those who live it, well aware of the risks. And so the murders of three hookers, strangled and dumped on a hillside in October 1977, elicited little more than a ripple.

But if police and the media were blasé about those crimes, they'd soon have cause to pay attention. Close to Thanksgiving 1977, came a week of unprecedented carnage. Within just a few days, the bodies of five young women were found in the vicinity of Glendale-Highland Park. These were not prostitutes, but ordinary girls, abducted from their middle-class neighborhoods, raped and tortured, then strangled and dumped in the hills.

The city was stunned, the media sparked into a frenzy of graphic reportage. The term "Hillside Strangler" was coined and entered

everyday conversation. A serial killer was on the loose. Or rather, a
pair of serial killers, because experienced detectives believed right
from the start that they were looking for two men, working
together.

On November 20, 1977, LAPD homicide Detective Bob Grogan was
called to the site of a murder, on a hillside somewhere between
Glendale and Eagle Rock. The victim was Kristina Weckler, a 20-
year-old honors student at the Pasadena Art Center of Design.
She'd been raped and sodomized and then strangled. The ligature
marks on her wrists, ankles, and neck, and the bruises on her
breasts, bore witness to torture.

While Grogan examined the crime scene, his partner, Dudley
Varney, had been called to another gruesome find, two victims this
time, their bodies in the early stages of decomposition, already
infested with insects. The victims would later be identified as
Dolores Cepeda and Sonja Johnson, just 12 and 14 years old
respectively. They'd last been seen getting off a bus and going over
to talk to a man sitting in a large sedan. Witness reports - that
there was a person on the passenger side of the vehicle -
supported the police theory that there were two killers.

Then, on November 23, another young woman's body was found,
this time near the Los Feliz off ramp on the Golden State Freeway.
The level of decomposition suggested that she'd been there two
weeks but made it impossible to determine whether she'd been
raped. But she had been strangled, and her wrists and ankles bore
the same ligature marks as the other victims. She was 28-year-old
Jane King, a model and actress. She'd been an attractive and

vibrant blonde before the strangler had snuffed out her life.

With the body count mounting, the LAPD, Glendale PD, and L.A. County Sheriff's Department (not always the best of friends) knew that they had to work together. A task force comprising 30 officers was established and was soon overwhelmed with tip-offs and suggestions from concerned citizens.

There were no further discoveries over the holiday weekend, but on Tuesday, November 29, the naked body of a young woman was found lying partially in the road in Glendale's Mount Washington area. The ligature marks on her ankles, wrists, and neck marked her out as a Hillside Strangler victim. There was evidence of torture too, including burn marks on her palms.

The young victim was identified as Lauren Wagner, an 18-year-old student who lived in the San Fernando Valley. Her parents had woken that morning to find her car parked across the street with the door open. Questioning the neighbors, Lauren's father learned that one of them, Beulah Stofer, had witnessed Lauren's abduction, even though she hadn't realized it at the time.

Stofer said that she had seen Lauren pull up to the curb at around nine o'clock. A car had stopped beside her, boxing her in. Two men got out of the vehicle and there was an altercation during which Stofer heard Lauren shout: "You won't get away with this!" Then Lauren left with the men.

Stofer had gotten a good look at the abductors and their car. The vehicle was a large sedan, dark in color with a white top. The men were Latin-looking, one tall and young with acne scars; the other, older and shorter, with bushy hair. She was sure that she would be able to identify the men if she saw them again.

The information was valuable, but the killing of Lauren Wagner posed a new problem for investigators. Previously the killers had confined their activities to Hollywood and Glendale. With this murder, they were spreading their wings. It seems they now regarded the entire city as their hunting ground. Nobody knew where the stranglers would strike next.

With no new leads to follow, detectives revisited the three prostitute murders with which the stranglers had announced their deadly presence. The first to die had been Yolanda Washington. Her raped and strangled body had been found near the Forest Lawn Cemetery on October 17, 1977.

Two weeks later, L.A. County Deputies responded to a report regarding the body of a young woman discovered in La Crescenta, a town just north of Glendale. The victim was Judith Miller, a 15-year-old prostitute who usually worked a beat along Hollywood Boulevard. Detectives soon found a witness who claimed to have seen Judith getting into a car with two men. He said he'd know them if he saw them again. But the prospects of solving the murder didn't look good. The only other clue was a tiny piece of fluff, found clinging to the victim's eyelid. This was later identified as the material used in the manufacture of car seats.

On November 6, 1977, the body of another strangulation victim turned up in Glendale. She was Lissa Kastin, a 21-year-old waitress who had recently confided in her mother that she was in desperate need of money and might turn to prostitution. She had last been seen leaving the restaurant where she worked, at about 9 o'clock on the night of her death.

Following that murder had come the horrendous Thanksgiving week, leading to the formation of the Hillside Strangler task force. But the killers then went quiet, perhaps thinking there was too much heat. They lay low for two weeks, re-emerging in mid-December to murder blonde call girl, Kimberly Diane Martin.

Martin had worked for the Climax modeling agency. On the night she died, the agency had received a call beckoning her to Apartment 114 at 1950 Tamarind. She'd been found the next day, her body discarded on a steep hillside bordering Alvarado Street.

This time, the police had what looked like a couple of promising leads. However, neither of these checked out. The killer had called the escort agency from a pay phone at the Hollywood Public Library, and the apartment Kimberly Martin been summoned to, did not exist.

No significant progress was made through December and January, but there were no new murders either. Then, on Thursday, February 16, an attractive young woman by the name of Cindy

Hudspeth was killed. Like the other victims, she'd been raped and strangled. Then her body had been placed in the trunk of her car and pushed down a hillside on Angeles Crest. Ligature marks on the neck, wrists, and ankles confirmed her as a Hillside Strangler victim.

Police continued working the case. But as the months passed with no new leads, nor any more killings by the Hillside Strangler, the trail began to go cold, the activities of the task force were scaled down, detectives began working other cases.

Almost a year later, police in Bellingham, Washington received a missing persons report on two Western Washington University students, Karen Mandic and Diane Wilder. Officers working the case learned that the girls had accepted a house-sitting job from a friend of theirs, a security guard named Ken Bianchi. However, when officers called on Bianchi, he claimed to know nothing about it and insisted that he'd never even met the girls. He also offered an alibi for the night the that Karen and Diane went missing. He'd been at a Sheriff's Reserve meeting, he said.

Bellingham police chief, Terry Mangan, was less than convinced by Bianchi's explanation. Something about the man's demeanor just bothered him. And he became even more suspicious when he found that Bianchi hadn't attended the Sheriff's meeting, as he'd claimed. Then, a search of the girls' apartment turned up the address of the Bayside residence the two had been hired to house-sit. A check on the security company's records showed that Kenneth Bianchi was responsible for the property. The police also noted that Karen Mandic's car was missing and learned that, on the night of the disappearance, Bianchi had signed out a company truck, supposedly to take it in for repair. Except, he'd never done so.

Concerned now that the girls might have come to harm, Chief Mangan asked the Highway Patrol to look for sites where a car might have been dumped. When that didn't produce a result, he turned to the media and arranged for them to broadcast photographs of the missing girls and a description of their vehicle.

Shortly after, a tip was called in by a woman who said that a car had been abandoned in a heavily wooded area near her home. Police rushed to the scene and had their worst fears realized. Inside the car were the bodies of Karen Mandic and Diane Wilder. Both had been strangled.

While the murdered women were being taken to the morgue, Chief Mangan ordered that Kenneth Bianchi be brought in for questioning. Bianchi was quite happy to oblige. The well-groomed six-footer was friendly and articulate. He told officers that he lived with his girlfriend, Kelli Boyd, and their infant son, having moved from L.A. a year ago. Kelli was stunned that someone as gentle-natured as Ken was being questioned about a double homicide. Bianchi's employee, too, had nothing but good things to say about him.

Bellingham police, though, were not taken in. They were convinced that Bianchi knew more than he was saying and were sure that the forensic evidence they'd gathered would implicate him. But they weren't ready to charge him with murder yet. What they needed was an excuse to take him into custody. Fortunately, Bianchi made it easy for them. The police found stolen items at his home – items he'd pilfered from the properties he was supposed to be protecting.

With their chief suspect now behind bars, the police stepped up their efforts in building a case against him. But something about the investigation still bothered Chief Mangan, and he soon realized what it was. The way the Bellingham victims had been tied up reminded him of a story he'd followed closely in the media - the Hillside Strangler murders. It had also not escaped his notice that Bianchi had moved to Washington a year ago, at around the time the Strangler murders had abruptly stopped. That rankled with the veteran investigator, so he decided to place a call to the L.A. County Sheriff's Office. Detective Frank Salerno was very interested in what he had to say.

The Hillside Strangler case had, by now, ground to a halt for lack of evidence. But the call from Bellingham got Salerno poring over old clues and he soon discovered something interesting. Kenneth Bianchi had lived close to three of the victims. Salerno immediately assigned detectives to check into Bianchi's activities in L.A. In the meanwhile, he hopped a plane to Washington to question the suspect. By the time he arrived, items of jewelry found in Bianchi's possession had been matched to distinctive pieces worn by two of the Hillside Strangler victims.

The case was building and it gained further momentum when L.A.

investigators released Bianchi's picture to the media and made an appeal for information. Within hours, they got a call from a lawyer named David Wood. Wood said that he'd once rescued two girls from Bianchi and his cousin, Angelo Buono, who had forced the young women into prostitution. He described Buono as vulgar, brutal, and sadistic, with a pathological hatred of woman.

Based on the tip-off, detectives paid Buono a visit and soon decided that he fit the profile. In fact, they were almost certain that this crude, ugly man, was the other Hillside Strangler.

Except, believing it and proving it were two different things and neither Kenneth Bianchi nor Angelo Buono was talking. Bianchi, in fact, was already working on an insanity defense. The idea had probably been planted in his head by a psychiatric social worker. Having examined Bianchi, the man commented that he couldn't understand how someone so mild-mannered could have strangled two women – unless he was suffering from multiple personality disorder.

Bianchi immediately jumped on this idea. He'd recently watched the movie Sybil, about a woman with multiple personalities. Drawing on the film, he created an alter ego, Steve Walker, who he claimed had committed the murders in L.A. and Washington. When Bianchi's defense attorney arranged for him to be interviewed by Dr. John G. Watkins, a renowned expert on multiple personalities, Watkins was convinced that Bianchi was an authentic case. So too was a court-appointed psychiatrist, Dr. Ralph Allison.

Prosecutors, though, had no intention of letting Bianchi's insanity defense go unchallenged. Dr. Martin Orne, an authority on hypnosis, was called in to determine if Bianchi was genuine. Orne had developed procedures to discover whether a subject was actually hypnotized or was just pretending to be. Bianchi's responses proved conclusively that he was faking.

With his insanity defense blown, the L.A. County District Attorney offered Bianchi a deal - plead guilty and testify against Buono and in exchange prosecutors would not seek the death penalty and would allow him to serve his time in California rather than at Washington's tough Walla Walla prison. Bianchi agreed.

Over the next weeks, Bianchi described to investigators how he and Buono had abducted, raped, tortured, and strangled their victims before dumping their bodies. They often posed as police officers to convince victims to go with them, he said. The unfortunate women were taken to Buono's auto upholstery shop, where they were subjected to a horrific ordeal. With neither remorse nor emotion, Bianchi described the brutal torture inflicted on their victims – sodomy, electric shocks, gassing, injections with acid-based cleaners, rape with various objects including soda bottles. The descriptions sickened even hardened detectives. Bianchi seemed entirely unmoved.

Based on his confession, Bianchi received two life sentences in the state of Washington. He was then transferred to California where he was sentenced to additional life terms. Now it was time to bring his brutal cousin, Angelo Buono, to justice.

Buono was arrested on October 22, 1979. Prosecutors believed that it would be a simple case, bolstered by Bianchi's testimony and supported by physical evidence and eyewitness reports of the various abductions. It was anything but simple.

First, Bianchi refused to co-operate, claiming amnesia and constantly changing his story. Then the prosecutor decided that, given Bianchi's antics, he wanted to drop the charges against Buono, a move which Judge Ronald George flatly refused. Following the judge's decision, the L.A. District Attorney's office withdrew from the case and a special investigator was appointed.

Finally, in November 1979, the case went ahead, to be immediately bogged down by continuances, motions, and a protracted jury selection process. The first evidence was only presented in the spring of 1982.

When the time came for Bianchi to testify, he was in no mood to co-operate. That is until the no-nonsense Judge George stepped in. He informed Bianchi that his lack of cooperation amounted to violating his plea-bargain, which meant that he would be sent to serve his time in the uncompromising environment of Walla Walla. Bianchi quickly fell into line.

On October 21, 1983, after what was - at the time - the longest criminal trial in U.S. history, the matter went to the jury. Ten days later, they delivered a guilty verdict in the Lauren Wagner case, and over the following days found Buono guilty of all but the Yolanda Washington murder. That meant that Buono faced either the death penalty or life in prison without possibility of parole. General consensus, given the horrendous nature of the crimes, was that he was destined for the gas chamber. But the jury inexplicably opted for the latter, clearly annoying the judge, who said as much in his summing up.

Angelo Buono was sent initially to Folsom Prison, where he reportedly refused to leave his cell, so afraid was he of being attacked by other inmates. He died of an apparent heart attack on September 21, 2002.

Kenneth Bianchi was held accountable for his lack of cooperation and his plea bargain was voided. Despite his protestations, he was sent to serve his sentence at Walla Walla. At the time of writing, he is still there.

David & Catherine Birnie

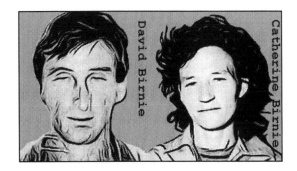

On the afternoon of November 10, 1986, a half-naked teenaged girl stumbled into a supermarket in Willagee, Western Australia, sobbing that she had been abducted and raped. The police were called and immediately rushed to the scene, where they found a hysterical 16-year-old, clearly traumatized by her ordeal. The girl was taken to Palmyra police station. After being attended by a doctor, she settled down enough to tell her extraordinary tale.

She said that she'd been walking near her home in Nedlands the previous evening when a man and woman stopped to ask for directions. While she was talking to them, the man got out of the car holding a large knife. He forced her into the vehicle, and she was then driven to a dilapidated house in Willagee. There, the couple tore off her clothes and chained her to a bed. The man then raped her, an action he'd repeat several more times over the course of the night, each time with the woman watching on impassively.

The following morning, the man left the house and the woman unchained her and took her to a phone. She was instructed to call her parents, to tell them that she was okay and was staying with friends. After she made the call, the woman left her unattended in order to answer a knock at the front door. Sensing her chance at freedom, the girl jumped from a bedroom window and escaped.

The police were very interested in the teenager's story. Over the previous few weeks, they had been investigating the disappearances of four young women from the streets of Perth. They'd begun to suspect that a serial killer might be at work. Could this case possibly be connected to the others?

Despite her ordeal, the girl clearly remembered the location of her abductors' house. She led the police to a rundown bungalow at number 3 Moorhouse Street, Willagee. No one was home, so detectives staked out the dwelling from a van parked across the road. They were soon rewarded when a slim woman with long, dark hair approached and slotted a key into the front door. She was arrested at the scene and later identified as Catherine Margaret Birnie. Her common-law husband, David John Birnie, was picked up at his place of work a short while later.

At first, the Birnies vigorously denied the girl's allegations, insisting that she'd smoked marijuana with them and that the sex had been consensual. However, detectives suspected that David Birnie might crack if additional pressure were applied. They kept at him for hours until he eventually broke down and admitted that he had abducted and raped the girl. Then he stunned his interrogators by also confessing to four murders. When Catherine Birnie heard of her husband's confession, she too began talking, eventually agreeing to take detectives to the burial sites of their victims.

That same evening the despicable couple led the Perth police to four shallow graves, three of them in Gleneagles National Park near Armadale, a fourth in Gnangara pine plantation, north of the city. It was only then that the police appreciated the brutality of the killer couple's murder spree. Three of the victims had been strangled; the fourth had been savagely stabbed and then hacked to death with an axe.

David John Birnie was born in Perth, Australia on February 16, 1951, the eldest of six children. His family was highly dysfunctional, their living conditions squalid, the parents both alcoholics, and the children placed in state care on numerous occasions. Left mainly unsupervised as a child, David attracted trouble early in life. Convicted on a catalog of felonies and misdemeanors, he was in and out of reform schools.

The opportunity to change all that came in 1966, when the 15-year-old David was recommended to Eric Parnham's stables as an apprentice jockey. The boy showed early promise, even if his cruel treatment of the horses raised alarm. He also could not seem to stay out of trouble and after his third arrest for robbery, Parnham Stables decided to cut their losses. David's apprenticeship was terminated. His dream of becoming a jockey was over.

But by now, David had developed a new hobby. He was addicted to pornography, an obsession that led him to commit his first rape, breaking into a home and forcing himself on an elderly woman. He was just 16 at the time. After quitting school, he found work at a motor scrapyard and, in his early 20s, he married and fathered a baby girl. However, the union soon floundered due to domestic violence and David's extreme sexual demands.

Catherine Birnie (nee Harrison) had endured a similarly difficult childhood. Also born in 1951, she lost her mother when she was just two years old. Her father then moved to South Africa, taking Catherine with him. Two years later, he sent her back to Australia, entrusting her to the custody of her maternal grandparents.

Catherine first met David Birnie when she was 12 years old, and the two were involved in a sexual relationship by the time she was 14. They then entered into a criminal partnership, carrying out a robbery spree, which eventually saw David sentenced to jail time and Catherine placed on probation. Her family used this opportunity to convince her to break ties with him, which she did, obtaining a position as housekeeper to the McLaughlin family. Over time, she became involved in a relationship with Donald McLaughlin, son of her employer, and the two married on Catherine's 21st birthday.

Catherine and Donald would have six children together, but Catherine had never forgotten David Birnie, and four weeks after the birth of her last child, she abandoned her family to be with him. She later took the Birnie name by deed poll and although they were never legally married, she and David lived together as man and wife.

The Birnie household was far from normal. David Birnie had a voracious sexual appetite, demanding intercourse as many as six times a day. He was heavily into kinky sex and had a succession of sexual partners, all of whom Catherine appears to have tolerated. So devoted was she to her man that when he first floated the idea of abducting and raping women, she was willing to go along. Whether or not she initially agreed to murder is not known.

The first killing took place on October 6, 1986. On that day, Birnie lured 22-year-old student Mary Neilson to his home with the promise of selling her some cheap tires. Once there, Mary was forced into the house at knifepoint, bound, gagged and chained to a bed. Birnie then repeatedly raped her, while Catherine watched.

That same night, the couple drove Mary to the Gleneagles National Park where Birnie again raped her. He then pulled a nylon cord around her neck and strangled her, using a tree branch to form a garrote. After Mary was dead, Birnie stabbed her in the chest (to release the gasses as the body decomposed, he told Catherine). Mary was consigned to a shallow grave before the depraved couple drove home.

The ease with which he had committed the first murder, encouraged Birnie to do it again. A fortnight later, he and

Catherine abducted 15-year-old Susannah Candy as she hitchhiked along the Stirling Highway in Claremont. Susannah was taken back to their Willagee home where she was gagged, chained to the bed and raped. This time, Catherine Birnie participated in the sexual assault.

Afterwards, Birnie tried to strangle the girl but she struggled so vigorously that he was persuaded to abandon his efforts. He then forced sleeping pills down her throat and waited until she passed out. Then he handed the rope to Catherine and insisted that she strangle Susannah to prove her love for him. Catherine willingly obliged. Like Mary Neilson, Susannah Candy was buried in the State Forest.

On November 1, the Birnies were out trolling again when they came upon 31-year-old Noelene Patterson, stranded at the side of the highway after her car ran out of gas. Noelene was glad to accept a ride from the friendly couple. Once inside the car, David held a knife to her throat, and she was forcibly taken back to Moorhouse Street.

Following the same M.O. as in the previous crimes, Birnie gagged and chained the unfortunate woman and then subjected her to a series of sexual assaults. Unlike the other victims, though, he did not kill her immediately. Instead, he held her captive for the next three days.

It was clear that David was taken with Noelene and a jealous

Catherine eventually gave him an ultimatum. Either he killed Noelene, or she would do it herself. A short while later, Birnie drugged and then strangled Noelene Patterson. Her body joined the others at Gleneagles.

On November 15, 21-year-old Denise Brown was waiting for a bus outside the Stoned Crow Wine House in Fremantle when the Birnies stopped and offered her a lift. She ended up being forced back to Moorhouse Street, where she was gagged, chained, and raped.

The following afternoon Denise was drugged and then driven to the Wanneroo pine plantation, where Birnie raped her. He then dug a shallow grave and dragged Denise into it. His lust still not sated, he penetrated her again as she lay in the hole, this time plunging a knife into her neck while he was raping her. Presuming that the girl was dead, he and Catherine started covering her with dirt. While they were doing so, Denise sat up in the grave, whereupon Birnie struck her twice on the head with an axe. Their most grisly murder to date duly accomplished, the sickening duo drove home.

The Birnies had now killed four women in the space of just 39 days. And they would undoubtedly have continued had the brave teenager not escaped their clutches. Now they were in custody, and it was up to the courts to ensure they were never at liberty to kill again.

David Birnie made that easy for them, pleading guilty to four counts of murder and one count each of abduction and rape. He was sentenced to four consecutive terms of life imprisonment.

Birnie's first posting was to the maximum security Fremantle prison where, after suffering a number of vicious beatings at the hands of fellow inmates, he was placed in solitary confinement for his own protection. He was found dead in his cell at Casuarina Prison on October 7, 2005. He had committed suicide by hanging.

Catherine Birnie, meanwhile, had been sentenced to the same term as her lover and was serving her time at Bandyup Women's Prison. A petition for early release was refused in 2007. In 2010, the Attorney General revoked her right to future parole applications, meaning that she will spend the rest of her days behind bars.

Henry Lee Lucas & Ottis Toole

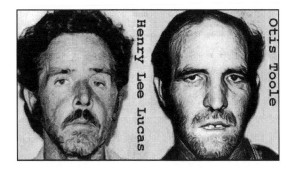

Depending on who you believe, Henry Lee Lucas is either the most prolific serial killer in American history or the most prolific liar. That Lucas was a murderer is beyond debate. He killed at least three women, making him a serial killer under the FBI's definition. But Lucas admitted at various times to over 3,000 murders, including one that put him on death row (and which he was later proven not to have committed). Even today, over a decade after his death, experts are divided. Many see him as a hoaxer, who'd confess to anything if it got him special treatment in jail. Others believe that he was indeed the killer he said he was, and may have been responsible for as many as 360 murders.

Lucas was born in a one-room log cabin in Blacksburg, Virginia, on August 23, 1936, the youngest of Viola and Anderson Lucas' nine children. His father was confined to a wheelchair, having lost both legs in a train accident; his mother was a half-Chippewa Indian, who made a living through prostitution and bootlegging. Viola was a cruel woman who was even meaner when she drank. According to Henry, she once beat him with a length of stove wood, putting him in a coma for three days. She also dressed him as a girl in order to humiliate him. When Henry sustained a serious eye injury at age 10, she refused to get treatment for him for four days, resulting in him losing the eye and having it replaced with a glass orb. On one occasion, she beat Henry for accepting a toy from one of his teachers, on another, she shot a mule that had been given to him by his uncle. If all of that were not bad enough, she liked to entertain her clients in front of her husband and children, beating the kids if they refused to watch.

In December 1949, Anderson Lucas got drunk and collapsed in the snow, resulting in him contracting a lethal case of pneumonia. Shortly after he died, Henry dropped out of school and ran away from home. He drifted around Virginia, surviving by committing burglaries and petty thefts. It was during this time, according to Lucas, that he committed his first murder, strangling 17-year-old Laura Burnsley, after she refused his sexual advances, and having sex with her corpse.

That story has never been verified (and Lucas later retracted the confession), but the following year, on June 12, 1952, he was in trouble when he was caught breaking into an appliance store. That earned him two years in a reformatory. Upon his release, he committed another break-in and was sent to the Virginia State Penitentiary for four years. During that incarceration, he managed to escape but was re-arrested and had five years tacked on to his sentence. He was released in 1959 and went to stay with his half-sister, Opal, in Tecumseh, Michigan.

In January 1960, Viola Lucas, aged 74 by now, came to visit and she and Henry began arguing about a woman Henry planned to marry. Viola insisted that he call the wedding off and move back to Blacksburg to look after her. The dispute continued, on and off, for several days until January 11. On that day, Henry and Viola had both been drinking and the argument soon turned violent with Henry stabbing his mother in the neck. Thinking he'd killed her, he fled the scene, but Viola was not dead. When Opal returned, she found her lying on the kitchen floor in a pool of blood. An ambulance was called but arrived too late.

Lucas was soon tracked down and put on trial for second-degree murder. He claimed he'd acted in self-defense but his claim was rejected, and he was given a sentence of 20 to 40 years' imprisonment. He served just ten before being paroled in June 1970.

After his release, Lucas moved to Pennsylvania where he got married in 1975. But the marriage soon broke down after Henry's wife accused him of molesting her young daughters. After that, Lucas took to drifting again, traveling throughout the American South, working at any number of low paying jobs. Eventually, he ended up in Jacksonville, Florida. It was there that he met the man with whom he'd form a deadly serial killer team, Ottis Toole.

Although most accounts cast Toole in Henry's shadow, his story is every bit as horrific as that of his sidekick. In fact, Toole, a serial killer and arsonist with an IQ just above mentally retarded, was arguably the more depraved of the duo.

Ottis Elwood Toole was born on March 5, 1947, in Jacksonville, Florida. Abandoned by his alcoholic father, he grew up in the custody of his religious fanatic mother, who he claims dressed him as a girl. Toole also claimed that his grandmother was a Satanist and that, as a child, he'd joined her on excursions to graveyards to dig up corpses for body parts. By his teens, Toole was already a serial arsonist who derived erotic pleasure from setting fires. He committed his first murder at 14, killing a traveling salesman who had convinced him to go into the woods with him for sex. The man made the grave mistake of leaving Toole alone while he went to relieve himself. As he emerged from the trees, Toole drove over him with his own car. By the time he met Lucas in 1976, Ottis Toole was already suspected of four murders.

The two misfits hit it off immediately and soon became homosexual lovers. Over the next four years, they traveled the country, visiting 26 states, committing murders wherever they landed. Their favorite victims were hitchhikers (female for Lucas, male for Toole), who they abducted, raped, and slaughtered, discarding their bodies along the side of the highway. Lucas would later claim that he and Toole committed 108 murders during this period.

In 1978, Toole introduced Lucas to his 12-year-old niece, Becky Powell. Lucas was instantly besotted and it wasn't long before he'd taken the child as his lover. For a time, the trio, along with Toole's nephew Frank, traveled together. Then, in 1981, Toole's mother died leaving him distraught and sparking a spell of heavy drinking and drug taking. On July 27 of that year, six-year-old Adam Walsh disappeared from a shopping mall. His head was found two weeks later in a canal ditch. Toole later claimed responsibility for the murder, an event that led to Adam's father, John Walsh, launching the television show, America's Most Wanted. (Toole's confession has since been broadly discredited)

In 1982, Lucas struck out on his own, taking Becky with him and leaving Ottis in the lurch. Angered by this desertion, Toole embarked on a 13-month killing spree that took him through six states and cost nine people their lives. He also revived his interest in arson and was caught setting a fire in Florida and sentenced to a 20-year jail term.

Lucas and Becky, meanwhile, had worked their way to Texas where they lived for a time with 82-year-old Kate Rich. However, Rich's family disliked Lucas and asked him to leave. He and Becky next found shelter at a Pentecostal commune near Stoneburg, Texas, known as the House of Prayer. The head of the group, Ruben Moore, gave Lucas and Becky a trailer to live in and found Lucas odd jobs in his construction business.

But Becky eventually grew homesick and wanted to return to Florida. Fearing that he'd lose her if she reunited with her family, Lucas resisted until August 24, 1982, when all of Becky's whining and nagging and crying eventually got to him and he relented. They set off the next day, hiking as far as Denton, Texas. While they were waiting for another ride, Lucas tried again to talk Becky out of the idea, but she was insistent and an argument ensued during which she slapped him. Angered, Lucas drew a knife and stabbed her in the chest, killing her instantly.

Henry claimed later that he was shocked and distraught at what he'd done. But that didn't stop him raping Becky's corpse right there beside the interstate (he said later that it was the best sex he'd ever had with her). He then dismembered the body, cutting it into nine pieces, which he scattered across a nearby field. He also dumped Becky's purse and small suitcase. After cleaning off her blood, he hitched a ride back to the House of Prayer where he told Ruben Moore that Becky had gone off with a trucker and left him. A couple of weeks later, Lucas returned to the field and buried Becky's remains in a shallow grave.

On September 16, about three weeks after Becky's death, Lucas arrived at Kate Rich's home in Ringgold. According to Lucas, he told Kate that he was going to look for Becky, and asked her to join him. Kate agreed and apparently didn't raise any questions about the butcher knife lying on the seat between them or the fact that Lucas was driving in the wrong direction.

Lucas said he was drinking beer as he drove, and suddenly hit on the idea of killing Kate. He turned onto a dirt road and drove a while before stopping the car. Without saying a word, he picked up the knife and stabbed Kate. He then got out of the car and walked around to the passenger side to finish the job. Kate, however, had sustained a wound to the heart and was already dead. Lucas then dragged the corpse down an embankment and had sex with it before concealing it in a drainage pipe.

The following day, Lucas left the House of Prayer and drove west, getting as far as Needles, California before his car broke down. After that, he drifted for about a month before returning to Kate's body. Removing the decomposing remains from the drainpipe, he took them back to the House of Prayer, where he disposed of them in a wood-burning stove.

Lucas was a suspect in the disappearances of both Becky and Kate, but when he was eventually arrested, on July 11, 1983, it was not for murder, but for illegal possession of a firearm. He was placed in a small cell in the Montague County jail where, according to Lucas, he was stripped naked and left without blankets and with the air-conditioning turned up. He was also denied cigarettes and refused access to a lawyer. After four days of this treatment, Lucas was ready to talk. "I done some bad things," he reportedly told one of his jailors. "I have been killing for the past ten years, and no one will believe me."

Investigators had hoped that Henry would confess to the murders of Kate Rich and Becky Powell and he did that, even leading them to the spot where Becky's dismembered corpse was buried. Then he provided directions to a storm water drain, where Kate Rich's bloodstained clothes and glasses were found. At the House of Prayer in Stoneburg, Lucas pointed out the stove where he'd incinerated Kate's remains and where a forensics team was able to recover scraps of bone and charred strips of human flesh.

Lucas was duly charged with two counts of murder and appeared for his arraignment at the Montague County Courthouse on June 21. It was here that he would drop the bombshell that would elevate him from run-of-the-mill homicidal hillbilly to arguably America's most infamous serial killer. "Yes, I killed Kate Rich," he told the packed courtroom, "and at least a hundred more beside."

Henry Lee Lucas had just admitted to being the most prolific murderer in American history, and the gathered press corps seemed to swallow it – hook, line, and sinker. By June 22, Lucas' admission had elevated him onto the front page of every newspaper in the nation.

Lucas, meanwhile, had written to Ottis Toole to tell him about Becky's death and to ask for his assistance in recalling details of the murders they had committed together. Toole wrote back forgiving his old partner and saying it was "Becky's time to go." He also offered details of two-dozen murders in 11 states and agreed that he and Lucas had claimed over 100 victims. The unholy pair were then allowed a phone call in which they discussed their crimes. They clearly enjoyed putting on a show for the listening officers, speaking of such repulsive acts as necrophilia and cannibalism. Most of those listening doubted that much of what they said was true. Nonetheless, they believed that Lucas and Toole could clear up a slew of open cases. By December 1983, a task force had been set up to do just that.

On December 7, 1983, Texas lawmen questioned Lucas about a catalog of unsolved homicides. Lucas had by this time confessed to 126 murders and been clearly linked to 35. In January 1984, 107 officers, from eighteen states, filled the Holidome in Monroe, Louisiana for a conference on the homicides allegedly committed by Lucas and Toole. Over three days, the officers believed they'd cleared 72 cases and linked the killer team to 70 more. Henry Lee Lucas had become the hottest law enforcement ticket in town, with officers from around the nation booking interviews with him to resolve their unsolved homicides.

In March 1984, Lucas eventually went on trial for one of the murders he was alleged to have committed. The victim was an unnamed young woman known only as Orange Socks, because that was the only item of clothing she had been wearing when found. The trial was in San Angelo, Texas, where the key piece of prosecution evidence was Lucas' tape recorded confession. In it, he described how he'd picked the woman up as a hitchhiker, had sex with her, killed her, had sex with her corpse, then dumped her in the culvert, skinning his knee on a guard rail in the process. On the same tape, Lucas can be heard claiming 360 murders. "We killed 'em most every way there is except poison," he boasted.

Whether that was true or not, the jury believed that there was sufficient evidence to convict Lucas of the 'Orange Socks' murder. The sentence of the court was death, an outcome that appeared hardly to ruffle the accused. Indeed, he seemed almost happy about it.

Yet, even as Lucas was being transported to death row, doubts were beginning to surface about his confessions. By now, he was claiming 600 victims in 27 different states and in Canada. And he was talking about being a member of a satanic execution cult called the Hands of Death. It was starting to sound more and more like a hoax.

And if law enforcement officers had been more attentive they'd have realized that Lucas could not have committed most of the crimes he was laying claim to. In many cases, he'd been out of state or in prison. Lucas himself added to the confusion by admitting to a Fort Worth reporter that he'd exaggerated his numbers. Indeed, some were beginning to think that he was only responsible for three murders – his mother, Becky Powell, and Kate Rich.

Officers who interviewed Lucas, meanwhile, insisted that he knew key unpublished details about the crimes and crime scenes. Lucas provided a ready explanation for that. He said that the Texas Rangers had given him everything he needed to base his confessions on, including photos and murder dockets. In some cases, they'd even taken him to the crime scenes. Lucas got to repeat these allegations in a live Good Morning America interview, throwing the entire case into disarray. The media called a hoax and Lucas' status changed overnight from one of the world's most notorious serial killers to one of the world's biggest liars.

No sooner had the dust settled than Lucas changed his story again. Appearing on radio on April 29, he insisted that he had murdered over 300 people. But by now, his credibility was blown. No one believed him anymore.

In June 1984, all investigations of open cases involving Lucas and Toole were halted, while many of the cases that had been "cleared" on Lucas' say-so were re-opened. Lucas was transferred to the state prison at Huntsville, bragging that he would be free within a month.

In 1991, Ottis Toole received four more life sentences for the murders of three women and a man in Florida between 1980 and 1981. Lucas was also charged but was not brought to Florida to face trial. Five years later in 1996, Toole died in prison from cirrhosis of the liver. That same year, Lucas' death sentence in the Orange Socks case came up for review.

Lucas was a lot less flippant at that hearing than he'd been at the original trial, breaking down in tears as he took the stand to recant his confession. He only knew about the murder, he said, because he had read the case file. In fact, he had an alibi – he'd been in Florida at the time. The result was a stay of execution, and Lucas' reprieve was complete two years later, when Texas Governor George W. Bush commuted his sentence to life in prison. It was the only death penalty (out of 153) that Bush overturned during his governorship.

No one knows exactly how many murders Henry Lee Lucas and Ottis Toole committed. Lucas certainly killed three and was ultimately convicted of 11. Toole may have killed more than that, and they undoubtedly committed murders as a team. The prevailing view among law enforcement professionals is that the number is likely to be in the 40 to 50 range. Few believe it to be as high as the 360 they claimed.

Henry Lee Lucas died in prison of natural causes in March 2001.

Gerald and Charlene Gallego

If ever a man was born to be a criminal, it was Gerald Armond Gallego. Gallego entered the world in 1946. Nine years later, his father, who he would never meet, was executed in Mississippi's gas chamber for the murder of two police officers. His mother, Lorraine Pullen Gallego, was a prostitute and drug addict. Gerald was raised by an extended family that included murderers and child molesters.

In contrast to Gerald's sordid upbringing, Charlene Gallego (nee Williams) had an idyllic childhood. Born in 1956 to Charles and Mercedes Williams, Charlene grew up in upper-middle-class Arden, Sacramento. Her father was a senior executive for a national grocery chain, and Charlene lacked for nothing. She was a bright student with a reported IQ of 160 and a talent for the violin.

But all of that changed when Charlene entered high school. Kids often act out during adolescence, but Charlene's fall from grace was spectacular. She started hanging out with a bad crowd and developed a taste for alcohol, drugs, and sex. Unsurprisingly, her grades slipped. Despite her obvious intelligence, she barely graduated.

Charlene's parents were quite obviously distressed by the chaotic path their daughter's life had taken. They consoled themselves with the belief that, having sown her wild oats, Charlene would mature and settle down. But if that was their expectation, they were to be sorely disappointed. Barely into her twenties, Charlene had already accumulated two failed marriages. And it would be all downhill from there.

By the time Charlene met Gerald Gallego in 1977, her husband-to-be had been arrested on no fewer than 23 occasions and had served time in a range of correctional facilities. He'd also been married and divorced five times. Gallego, it seemed, was irresistibly attractive to a certain type of woman, and Charlene definitely came into that category.

The appeal was apparently mutual. Within days of their initial meeting, Gerald sent Charlene a dozen roses. A few weeks later they had moved in together. But if Charlene had any illusions about how the relationship was going to be, Gerald soon dispelled them. She was to be the breadwinner, but all of her paychecks were to be handed directly to him. He would tell her what to wear and how to behave. He'd also openly conduct affairs with other women, whether she liked it or not.

Given these conditions, the strong-willed Charlene might have been expected to walk out the door without looking back. But she didn't. Even when Gerald floated the idea of abducting young girls and using them as sex slaves, she stayed. The scheme appealed to her. It sounded exciting and dangerously intriguing.

On September 11, 1978, Gerald declared that it was time to put his plan into action. He told Charlene to drive their Dodge panel van to the Country Club Plaza shopping center. Once there, he instructed her to wander around the mall until she found two suitable sex slaves. She was then to lure them back to the van.

Charlene hesitated at first. The idea had sounded fine in principle, but she wasn't sure that she could carry it out. She was afraid of being arrested, unsure whether she could really coax two girls back to the van where they faced an almost certain death. On the other hand, she knew what Gerald's reaction would be if she failed him. Caught on the horns of a dilemma, Charlene did what she always did. She did what Gerald told her to do.

Cruising the mall, Charlene soon found two likely candidates. Rhonda Scheffler, 17, and Kippi Vaught, 16, were doing some shopping when Charlene approached and asked if they wanted to smoke some pot. The girls were immediately interested. Charlene looked much younger than her years, about their own age, and she seemed friendly. What was the worst that could happen?

That question was answered for them the minute the van's door slid open, and they found themselves face to face with Gerald Gallego, brandishing a .25-caliber pistol. The girls were easily subdued, bound and thrown into the back. While Charlene held the gun on them, Gerald drove east on I-80 toward the Sierra Nevada Mountains. He left the interstate at Baxter, drove to an isolated spot and then forced the girls out at gunpoint. Then he told Charlene to wait in the vehicle while he walked into the bushes with Rhonda and Kippi. A few hours later, he returned, forcing the girls in front of him at gunpoint. He then told Charlene to drive back to Sacramento, and to visit some friends while she was there, in order to establish an alibi. She was then to drop off the van and return to pick him up in the couple's Oldsmobile.

Charlene did as she was told. She returned to find Gerald waiting by the side of the road with his captives. He forced the girls into the back seat of the Olds and told Charlene to drive. Some fifteen minutes later, he brought her to a stop along an isolated stretch of road where he ordered Rhonda and Kippi from the vehicle. Perhaps realizing what was about to happen, they began to cry, to beg for their lives. It did them no good. They were battered into submission with a tire iron and then finished off with a bullet to each of their heads.

The disappearance of two young girls from a busy shopping mall caused a lot of heat in Sacramento. Perhaps sensing that he'd eventually end up on the suspect list due to his long police record, Gerald decided that it might be a good idea to skip town for a while. The couple fled to Reno where they obtained a quickie marriage and then moved to Houston, where Charlene's father had organized a truck driving job for Gerald. But Gerald hated Texas and particularly hated the idea of having to work for a living.

Within a year, he and Charlene had moved back to Reno. Not long after their arrival, Gerald announced that he was ready to hunt again.

On June 24, 1979, the Gallegos drove to a fair in Washoe County, Nevada where they followed their familiar M.O. The victims, this time, were even younger, 14-year-old Brenda Judd and 13-year-old Sandra Colley. Charlene approached the girls and asked if they were interested in making some money by helping her distribute advertising flyers. The girls said that they were, and followed Charlene back to the van, where Gerald waited.

Brenda and Sandra were easily overpowered. Then, as the van sped away from the fairground with Charlene at the wheel, Gerald got into the back and sexually assaulted the terrified girls. Somewhere along I-80, he ordered Charlene to stop at a hardware store and pick up a hammer and a shovel. Then they drove on, heading into the desolate Nevada Hills. Brenda Judd and Sandra Colley were raped and then bludgeoned to death with a hammer. Their bodies were laid to rest in the sandy ground beside a dirt road.

The disappearances of Brenda and Sandra caused a considerable uproar. But the police had little to go on, and the investigation soon ground to a halt. Gerald, nonetheless, had decided that it was time to return to Sacramento, which they did, arriving in late 1979.

For a few months, things returned to what passed for normality in the Gallego household. Charlene found a job while Gerald stayed home drinking beer and watching TV. He also took a succession of lovers, beating Charlene if she raised any objection. Then, in April 1980, he decided that it was time to find some new sex slaves.

On April 24, the Gallegos drove their van to the Sunrise Mall in Citrus Heights, some 20 minutes outside of Sacramento. There, following their usual routine, they captured Stacey Ann Redican and Karen Twiggs, both seventeen. Charlene then drove a familiar route along I-80 while Gerald repeatedly raped the teenagers in the back of the van. Eventually, they ended up at Limerick Canyon near Lovelock, where the girls were beaten to death with a hammer.

The Gallegos by now had a well-established routine. But in June 1980, they deviated from it, committing a murder on the spur of the moment. They were vacationing in Oregon when they spotted Linda Aguilar walking along the highway. She wasn't exactly Gerald's type, too old for one thing at 21, dark haired, and also pregnant. However, Gerald stopped the van and offered her a ride and Linda accepted.

They hadn't gone far before Gerald stopped and told Charlene to take the wheel. Then he forced Linda into the back and raped her, while Charlene continued driving, looking for a suitable spot to dispose of the body. Eventually, she drove into the woods, where Gerald ordered Linda from the van, then clubbed her with a rock and strangled her to death.

A month later, back in Sacramento, Gerald and Charlene committed an even more audacious murder. Virginia Mochel was a bartender at the Sail Inn, a West Sacramento tavern where the Gallegos often drank. Gerald had developed an infatuation with the attractive 34-year-old but after having his advances rebuffed, he decided to take what he wanted by force. Virginia was abducted, driven to a field outside Clarksburg, and there raped and murdered.

For the first time, the Gallegos had targeted a victim who could be connected to them, and they soon found detectives knocking at their door. However, they denied any involvement in Virginia Mochel's disappearance and with no evidence to prove otherwise, the police were forced to let things drop.

The investigation had put a strain on the relationship, though. Charlene, who had been against the killing of Virginia Mochel, accused Gerald of putting their lives in jeopardy. He responded by delivering yet another beating and this time Charlene had finally had enough. She moved in with her parents, leaving Gerald in the lurch. He initially seemed unconcerned and took up with an old flame. But he was soon pining for his warped partner in love and murder. He began pestering Charlene with phone calls and cards, begging for another chance, swearing that he'd change. Charlene, as always a sucker for his dubious charms, agreed to see him.

On November 1, Charlene borrowed her father's Oldsmobile, saying that she and Gerald were going to a movie. Instead, they went out drinking, and once Gerald was drunk, he started reminiscing about old times and suggesting that they go cruising for sex slaves. Charlene agreed. Before long, they were trawling shopping center parking lots, looking for likely victims.

The plan once again deviated from their tried and tested methodology but they'd both had a lot to drink, and they were reckless. At the Arden Fair Center, Gerald suddenly shouted to Charlene to stop the car. He then jumped from the vehicle and accosted Craig Miller and Mary Elizabeth Sowers, forcing them at gunpoint into the Oldsmobile. Unbeknownst to the Gallegos, a friend of Craig's had spotted the abduction, and as they sped off, he jotted down the license plate number. He then ran for a phone to call the police.

An alert was immediately issued to all patrol cars to be on the lookout for the Oldsmobile. Unfortunately, it was not enough to save Craig Miller and Mary Beth Sowers. Craig was executed by three bullets to the head. Mary Beth was taken back to Gerald Gallego's apartment where she was brutally raped while Charlene watched TV in the next room. Then she too was shot, her body driven into the country and dumped in a field.

In the meanwhile, the police had traced the Oldsmobile to Charlene's father and roused him in the early morning hours with some disturbing news about his daughter. When Charlene returned the car the next morning, the police were waiting. Gerald however, had spotted the cruisers parked outside his in-law's residence and had instructed Charlene to drop him off. He promptly went into hiding, leaving Charlene to face the music alone.

Charlene, however, was no pushover. Under intense questioning, she stuck to the story that she and Gerald had gone to a movie the previous night and had not been driving the Oldsmobile but a red Triumph that belonged to one of Gerald's friends. The friend, conveniently, was out of town, and Charlene said that she did not know how to reach him. The police were forced to back off while they verified the alibi. As soon as they were gone, Charlene hooked up with Gerald and the couple skipped town, driving first to Reno, then ditching their car and boarding a bus for Salt Lake City.

Back in Sacramento, the police were building a strong case against the Gallegos. Craig Miller's friend identified a picture of Gerald as the man who'd abducted Craig and Mary Beth. And Craig's body had been found, the bullets that had killed him matched to Gerald Gallego's .25. Detectives had enough evidence to charge the fugitives. All they had to do was find them.

The break came when Charlene phoned her father from Omaha, Nebraska and asked him to wire her some money. Charles Williams did as he was asked, but he passed the information to the FBI. When Gerald and Charlene arrived at the Western Union office, agents were waiting for them.

Faced with the prospect of a death sentence for her part in the murders, Charlene quickly struck a deal. She agreed to testify against Gerald in exchange for a prison term of sixteen years and eight months, the minimum for first-degree murder in California. She made a similar deal with the Nevada authorities. Gerald

Gallego was on his own now, and with Charlene's testimony against him, he was very likely to face the death penalty.

And so it proved. Convicted of the murders of Craig Miller and Mary Beth Sowers in California, Gallego was sentenced to die. A similar result followed from his Nevada trial, for the murders of Stacy Redican, Karen Twiggs, Brenda Judd, and Sandra Colley.

But Gallego would never keep his date with the executioner. While incarcerated at Nevada's Ely State Prison, he contracted rectal cancer, which spread to his liver and lungs. He died on July 18, 2002, at the age of 56.

Charlene Gallego was released from a Nevada prison in July 1997 and promptly disappeared. Her current whereabouts are unknown.

Viktor Sayenko & Igor Suprunyuck

The Eastern European nation of Ukraine has produced some of the world's most depraved killers, not least the 'Rostov Ripper,' Andrei Chikatilo, a necrophile and cannibal who slaughtered at least 50 women and children in a reign of terror lasting from 1978 to 1990. But not even Chikatilo can match the sheer ferociousness of the murder spree perpetrated by Viktor Sayenko and Igor Suprunyuck. In the space of just three weeks, from June 25 to July 16, 2007, these teenaged psychopaths claimed 18 victims, bludgeoning them so brutally that the corpses were rendered unrecognizable. And to add an extra level of depravity, they videotaped some of the murders, even posting one on the Internet.

Sayenko and Suprunyuck first became friends in the third grade.

They had a lot in common. Both were from wealthy and influential families. Suprunyuck's father was an air force officer and later the personal pilot of Ukrainian President Leonid Kuchmatwo; Sayenko's father was a high-profile lawyer, who would later represent his son during his murder trial.

How then did these two privileged, rich kids veer towards serial murder? It is difficult to say. Tracing their friendship to its earliest days, we find that they were a bad influence on each other from the very beginning. Sayenko had been a diligent student when they first met, while Suprunyuck had been shy and somewhat withdrawn. Together, though, they quickly veered towards trouble.

The boys' first brush with the law came when they were in the fifth grade. On that occasion, they were arrested for throwing rocks at passing trains but were released with a warning after Sayenko's father pulled some strings. Perhaps emboldened by this let off, they gravitated to other criminal acts. By the eighth grade, they were routinely torturing animals, a trait that has been noted in many fledgling serial killers. And they were recording many of these horrendously cruel acts on video, something that would later become part of their modus operandi.

Suprunyuck and Sayenko clearly considered themselves to be above the law. At 17, Sayenko beat up a boy in broad daylight and stole his bicycle in front of several witnesses. Inevitably, he was arrested and just as inevitably he walked on the charge. Someone without his connections would likely have ended up in a juvenile detention facility.

But the day was fast approaching when these callous youths would no longer be juveniles. Suprunyuck had never been much of a student and under his influence, Sayenko's academic performance had also dropped off significantly. Still, the pair somehow managed to graduate high school and thereafter drifted into menial jobs. Sayenko became a security guard; Suprunyuck used the Daewoo Lanos his parents had bought for him to operate an unlicensed taxi. He also supplemented his income by beating up and robbing his passengers. Soon he and his boyhood friend would gravitate towards even more serious crimes.

The murder spree that would eventually catapult Viktor Sayenko and Igor Suprunyuck to lasting infamy began late on the evening of June 25, 2007. Sayenko and Suprunyuck were out prowling the streets when they encountered 33-year-old Ekaterina Ilchenko, returning home after visiting a friend. Suprunyuck was carrying a hammer and without provocation, he suddenly attacked the woman, first striking her on the side of the head and then straddling her after she fell, raining down blow after blow on his hapless victim. By the time he and Sayenko walked laughing from the scene, Ekaterina Ilchenko's face had been reduced to a pulp of blood, brain matter, and splintered bone.

But still the bloodlust of these miscreants was not satisfied. Just an hour later, they found a vagrant named Roman Tatarevich asleep on a bench across the road from the Public Prosecutor's office. Tatarevich was beaten to death before he'd even had a chance to rise, his features rendered unrecognizable under the vicious onslaught.

Just six days later, on July 1, the psychopathic duo struck again, this time traveling to the nearby town of Novomoskovsk, where they left two victims, Evgeniya Grischenko and Nikolai Serchuk, bludgeoned to death.

In the early morning hours of July 6, Sayenko and Suprunyuck were again trawling the streets of their hometown when they encountered Egor Nechvoloda, somewhat the worse for wear, walking home from a nightclub. Without warning they attacked, battering the man to the ground and then kicking and beating him to death.

Egor Nechvoloda was just the first of three victims they'd claim that night. Twenty-eight-year-old Elena Shram was attacked and bludgeoned to death while working her shift as a security guard. Valentina Hanzha, a mother of three young children, met a similar fate just hours later.

With the media now widely reporting the vicious attacks carried out by the "Dnepropetrovsk Maniacs," Sayenko and Suprunyuck appeared next in the village of Podgorodnoye. There, they found two 14-year-old boys on their way to a fishing hole and attacked them, killing one of the children, Andrei Sidyuck. The other boy, Vadim Lyakhov, managed to escape and was able to provide police with their first description of the killers.

Not that it slowed the killing spree in any way. On July 12, 48-year-old Sergei Yatzenko went missing while riding his motorcycle near Dnepropetrovsk. His body was found four days later. He'd been savagely beaten to death.

Unlikely though it seems, given the ferocity of their initial spree, Sayenko and Suprunyuck now upped the tempo, committing thirteen murders over the next four days. Their victims seem to have been chosen at random and included women and children, the elderly, vagrants, and people who were under the influence of alcohol and therefore easy to subdue. The ferociousness of the attacks also increased. Many of the victims were mutilated and tortured, some had their eyes gouged out while they were still alive, a pregnant woman had the fetus ripped from her womb. Many of these vile acts were captured on video by the killers.

But Sayenko and Suprunyuck were already making a number of reckless mistakes, one of which would lead directly to their capture. With the later murders, they'd taken to robbing their victims of cash, cell phones, and other valuables. On July 23, 2007, Suprunyuck attempted to sell a mobile phone stolen from one of the victims at a local pawnshop. The pawnbroker insisted that he turn the phone on, to prove that it worked. Suprunyuck gladly agreed.

Unbeknownst to him, the police were monitoring the phone and once it was turned on, they were able to pinpoint its location. Officers raced to the scene and arrested Suprunyuck on site. He soon gave up his accomplice.

Under questioning both Sayenko and Suprunyuck quickly
confessed, although Suprunyuck later withdrew his statement.
Their trial, beginning in June 2008, was a media sensation in
Ukraine with the public astounded by the youthfulness and callous
indifference of these savage killers.

Much was made of the motive behind the murders. One of the
more outlandish theories was that Sayenko and Suprunyuck had
struck a deal with a wealthy snuff movie collector, whereby they
agreed to carry out and film 40 murders in exchange for a large
sum of money. Lead investigator Bogdan Vlasenko rejected this
idea. "We believe they did it as a hobby," he said. "To have a
collection of memories for when they get old."

Whatever the motive, there was little doubt as to the outcome of
the trial. Sayenko had, in fact, pleaded guilty in the hope of
receiving a lesser sentence, while Suprunyuck arrogantly
challenged the prosecutor to prove which of the two had struck
the killing blows.

In the end, it made no difference. On February 11, 2009, both
Viktor Sayenko and Igor Suprunyuck were found guilty on
multiple counts of murder. Since Ukraine has no death penalty
they were sentenced to life in prison.

Martha Beck & Raymond Fernandez

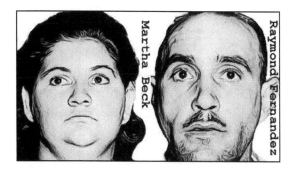

In July 1949, during one of the worst heatwaves of the 20th century, the city of New York was brought to a virtual standstill by the sensational trial of Raymond Fernandez and Martha Beck. Dubbed the Lonely Hearts Killers, the pair stood accused of killing 66-year-old Janet Fay in January of that year. As the trial continued, the shocked gallery would learn of three more murders, including that of a two-year-old baby.

But what was it that turned a toupee wearing, Latin lothario and his obese, lovesick girlfriend from small-time con artists into mass murderers? To find that out, we have to look back on their rather ill-fated histories.

Raymond Martinez Fernandez was born in Hawaii, on December 17, 1914. When he was three, his family moved to Bridgeport, Connecticut where he spent his childhood. Raymond was of

Spanish descent and returned to the home of his forefathers in 1932. There he worked on his uncle's farm and married a local woman, Encarnacion Robles, by who he later fathered a son. He was a handsome young man with a calm, gentle manner that made him well-liked around the village of Orgiva. During World War II, he served with the Spanish merchant marine and was also, apparently, a spy for the Allies.

When the war ended in 1945, Fernandez decided to return to America and found passage on a freighter bound for the island of Curacao in the West Indies. The idea was that he would go ahead to find work and then send for his wife and son. However, while on board the ship, Fernandez suffered a serious injury when a steel hatch struck him on the head. When the ship docked, he was taken to a hospital.

Fernandez would remain hospitalized until March 1946. After being discharged, he boarded a ship for Mobile, Alabama but fell into trouble with the law immediately after his arrival on US soil. He was found by customs officials to be in possession of stolen property and was arrested on the spot. Tried and found guilty, he was sentenced to a year at the federal penitentiary in Tallahassee, Florida.

While in prison, Fernandez shared a cell with a Haitian man who introduced him to the ancient religion of Vordun. It wasn't long before he'd developed an unhealthy obsession with the occult, drawing much of his doctrine from "The Black Republic," a sensationalist script that has many inaccuracies. Nonetheless, Fernandez bought into it. He began to believe that he had sexual power over women, that he was a voodoo priest, and that he could communicate with the spirits.

After his release from prison in 1946, Fernandez went to live with his sister in Brooklyn, New York. His relatives were shocked by his appearance. The once handsome Raymond was now gaunt and stooped, with a bald pate and an ugly scar that ran across his scalp. His behavior was also different. Once he'd been pleasant, courteous, and sociable. Now, he was irritable and quick to anger. Probably as a result of his head injury, he suffered from severe headaches that would keep him confined to his room for days.

It was around this time that Fernandez started writing to Lonely Hearts clubs, and soon he'd developed a neat little scam. He'd correspond with desperate spinsters and widows, gain their trust through his eloquent letters, and then arrange a meeting. After that, he'd con his way into their lives and then systematically embezzle them out of whatever cash and valuables they had. The victims were usually too embarrassed to go to the police.

One of the women dragged into Raymond's net of deceit was Jane Thompson. Fernandez met Jane in October 1947 and swept her off her feet. Within weeks, she'd paid for a cruise to Spain, and they traveled there as man and wife. Fernandez even introduced Jane to his real wife, and the three of them were often seen together, dining out and sightseeing.

But on November 7, 1947, an incident occurred that would bring

the budding relationship to an abrupt and tragic end. It appears
Raymond and Jane got into an argument. Raymond was seen
running from Jane's room late at night and the next morning the
woman was discovered dead. Suspicions of poisoning were raised,
but Raymond wasn't sticking around to answer questions. He
skipped town and got a ship back to New York. Once there he
produced a forged will and took possession of Jane Thompson's
assets, including her apartment, from which he evicted her elderly
mother.

Set up in his new home, Raymond Fernandez got back to writing
letters. One of them went to Martha Beck.

Martha Jule Seabrook was in born in Milton, Florida in 1919. As a
child, she developed a glandular condition that caused her weight
to balloon out of control. By the age of 10, she was already obese
and the subject of cruel jokes and taunts from her classmates.
Worse still were the insults that she had to endure from her
mother. By her teens, she'd become a virtual recluse, cut off from
her family and with no friends of her own age.

Martha, though, was made of stern stuff. After finishing high
school, she enrolled in nursing college, graduating in 1942 at the
top of her class. However, because of her appearance, she was
unable to find work in Florida, and she, therefore, decamped for
California and a job in a military hospital.

Martha was an excellent nurse, competent and decisive. After hours, though, it was a different story. Lonely and desperate for attention, she began hanging out in bars, picking up soldiers for casual sex. As a result of one of these encounters, she fell pregnant. When the father of the child denied paternity and refused to have anything to do with her, a heartbroken Martha returned home to Florida.

In 1944, Martha gave birth to a daughter. A few months later, she started dating a bus driver, Alfred Beck, and became pregnant again. She and Alfred were married in late 1944, but the marriage only lasted six months before ending in divorce.

In early 1946, Martha finally secured another nursing job - at the Pensacola Hospital for Children. There, she quickly proved her worth, gaining several promotions and eventually becoming head nurse of the hospital.

But she still found herself the butt of co-worker's cruel jibes and pranks. When one of those co-workers sent her details to a Lonely Hearts club as a joke, Martha defiantly decided to go ahead and join the club anyway. She placed an ad with "Mother Dinene's Family Club for Lonely Hearts," conveniently omitting the fact that she weighed nearly 250 pounds and already had two kids.

Martha may have entered the world of correspondence courtships by default, but it soon began to take over her life. Every day she would return from work and rush to the mailbox, hoping to find a letter from Mother Dinene's. But suitors were hardly beating a path to her door. Two weeks passed without a single reply. Then, just before Christmas Day in 1947, a letter arrived from Mr. Raymond Fernandez of New York City.

Fernandez, still working his well-worn scam, described himself as a respectable businessman involved in the import/export trade. His letter was articulate, courteous, and dripping with sincerity. To the love-starved Martha, it was like catnip to a kitten. She wrote back immediately and over the next two weeks they exchanged a dozen letters. When Fernandez asked for a photo, she sent a group shot, taken with colleagues at the hospital. She didn't want to scare him off.

But Martha's appearance was of little concern to Fernandez. He didn't care much what his victims looked like, as long as they had something he could steal. Martha, being a working woman, might have assets. If so, he was determined to relieve her of them.

And so it was that, after a couple of weeks of correspondence, Fernandez set off for Pensacola, Florida and a face-to-face meeting. He arrived on December 28, 1947, and Martha was at the station to meet him. She must have been nervous, he, perhaps, shocked by her massive size. If so, he'd have recovered his composure quickly. Raymond Fernandez was too experienced a conman to show any sign of disapproval.

For her part, Martha was instantly besotted with her toupee-wearing suitor. She took Raymond home to meet her children, prepared dinner for him and later, after the kids had been put to bed, she and Raymond had sex for the first time.

They spent the next couple of days together, during which Fernandez did an assessment of Martha's assets. Disappointed by the potential haul, he announced suddenly that he had to return to New York. When Martha begged him to stay, he said he had business to attend to, but promised to send money and a train ticket so she could join him later.

A couple of weeks later, Martha received a letter from Fernandez ending the relationship. She wrote back, threatening suicide. He responded, begging her to reconsider, if only for the sake of her children. She, encouraged, fired off another missive, declaring her eternal love. Perhaps flattered by this show of devotion, Fernandez eventually agreed to let her visit him.

Martha stayed in New York for two weeks, but when she returned to Florida, a surprise awaited her - she was fired from her job without explanation. She should have been devastated by this development, but instead, she was delighted. Without even consulting Fernandez, she packed up her kids and hopped a bus to New York, arriving on January 18, 1948.

Fernandez was less than delighted with this turn of events. He didn't mind having Martha around, but the children cramped his style. When he said as much to Martha, she barely put up a fight. The following day, January 25, 1948, she dropped her kids off at the Salvation Army. She would never see them again.

With the kids out of the way, Fernandez figured that, if Martha was going to stay, he was going to have to fill her in on some home truths. He told her about the scams he was running, about the dozens of lonely women he'd already deceived and robbed. His initial letter to her, he admitted, had been written with similar motivations in mind. Since then, however, he'd actually become quite fond of her.

Given these revelations, Fernandez might have expected Martha to walk out on him, but she did no such thing. Instead, she asked to participate in his next scam.

The victim they chose was Esther Henne, a widow from Pennsylvania. On February 21, 1948, Raymond and Martha traveled together to meet Mrs. Henne, Martha posing as Raymond's sister. Within the week, Esther Henne became Mrs. Raymond Fernandez. Soon after, Raymond started pressing her to sign her pension and insurance policies over to him. When she refused, Raymond and Martha absconded with her car and hundreds of dollars in cash.

Several other women were scammed in quick succession. One of them was Myrtle Young of Greene Forest, Arkansas. Fernandez married her in Illinois on August 14, 1948, after which Martha did everything she could to prevent the marriage from being consummated. When Myrtle complained, Raymond gave her a dose of sleeping pills, then robbed her of $4,000 and put her on a bus back to Arkansas. Myrtle was so heavily sedated that she had to be carried from the bus at Little Rock. She died in hospital the next day, the first victim of the "Lonely Hearts Killers."

Martha and Raymond, meanwhile, continued to run their scams and soon came across Janet Fay, a 66-year-old widow from Albany, New York. Using the alias Charles Martin, Fernandez began corresponding with Mrs. Faye in December 1948. On December 30, a meeting was arranged, Raymond arriving at Janet's door with a bouquet of flowers. Mrs. Faye was a church-going woman, and they spent the day together discussing mainly religious matters.

Over the next few days, Fernandez began bringing Martha along, introducing her as his sister. Soon Raymond proposed, and Janet accepted. During the first week in January 1949, Janet cleared out her bank accounts in Albany, withdrawing over $6,000. On January 4, she drove to Long Island with Fernandez and Beck.

When they arrived, they ate dinner together. Shortly afterward, Fernandez fell asleep – and woke to a commotion. He found Janet lying on the floor, bleeding from a severe head wound, Martha standing over the elderly woman with a hammer in her hand.

What actually happened will never be known. Martha would later admit that she'd been burning up with jealousy because of the amount of attention Raymond was showing Janet. She claims to have blacked out and woken up with Raymond shaking her and shouting, "Martha, what have you done?"

What Martha had done, was to club Janet Fay into a state of
unconsciousness. But Janet was still breathing. That is until Martha
tightened a tourniquet around her neck and she suffocated.
(Martha would would later claim that her intention was to stop the
bleeding from the head wound.)

With Janet now lying dead on the floor, Beck and Fernandez
sprung into action. They cleaned up the blood, wrapped the corpse
in some sheets, and stuffed it into a closet. The next day, they
bought a trunk, put the body inside and drove to Raymond's
sister's house. They convinced her to store the trunk in her
basement. Eleven days later, they retrieved the corpse and buried
it in the cellar of a house they'd rented.

Over the course of the next week, the killers cashed Janet Fay's
checks and typed letters to her family, keeping up the pretense
that she was still alive. They'd made a crucial mistake, though.
Janet Fay always corresponded by handwritten notes. She couldn't
type and didn't own a typewriter. Her family was immediately
suspicious and called the police.

But Beck and Fernandez had, by now, moved on to Grand Rapids,
Michigan. Fernandez, still using the alias Charles Martin, had been
corresponding with a 41-year-old widow named Delphine
Downing.

In late January 1949, "Charles Martin" called on Delphine. She was impressed by his good manners and his way with her two-year-old daughter, Rainelle. It wasn't long before they were sleeping together, something that incensed Martha. All of the women they'd targeted up till now had been elderly, but Delphine was middle-aged and still quite attractive. Martha began to fear that she might lose her man.

But Delphine's infatuation with "Charles" came to an abrupt end when she saw him one morning without his toupee. His bald head, with the ugly scar running across it, repulsed her, and she told him as much. An argument erupted during which Delphine called Fernandez a fraud and asked him to leave.

Martha, of course, was thrilled that the lovers had fallen out. But she had learned from her outburst with Janet Faye and was by now able to keep her emotions in check when the need arose. She took Delphine to one side, calmed her down and convinced her to take a couple of sleeping pills. It wasn't long before Delphine was snoring.

That, at least, bought Beck and Fernandez some time. What should they do now? Delphine was almost certain to throw them out once she woke up. They'd put weeks of work into the scam and were about to walk away with nothing to show for it.

It was Rainelle who forced the issue. When the little girl began crying for her mother, Martha reacted angrily, grabbing the child by the throat. She might well have throttled the life out of the two-year-old had Fernandez not intervened.

The damage, however, was done. Rainelle had ugly bruises on her neck, which Delphine was sure to notice. Then she'd call the police, and the game would be up. Fernandez was not about to let that happen. He fetched a handgun and placed the muzzle against the sleeping woman's temple. Then he pulled the trigger, killing her instantly. Later, he and Martha wrapped the body in sheets and buried it in the basement.

Over the next two days, Fernandez and Beck continued living in Delphine's house, cashing her checks and pawning anything of value. Then they were ready to leave, but they still had Rainelle to worry about.

According to Martha, it was Raymond's idea to kill the little girl, but it was Martha herself who committed the vile deed. She ran a tub full of water and held the two-year-old under until she drowned. Then they buried the child in the basement, next to her mother.

Fernandez and Beck might have made a clean getaway if they'd left immediately. Instead, the callous killers decided to go to a movie. They returned to find the police, summoned by concerned neighbors, waiting for them.

Arrested on February 28, 1949, Beck and Fernandez were more than willing to cooperate with Michigan authorities. The reason was simple. Michigan had no death penalty, and under assurances that they wouldn't be extradited back to New York, they made and signed full confessions.

However, as details of the Lonely Hearts murders exploded onto the front pages of the nation's newspapers, there was an enormous public outcry, a demand almost, that Beck and Fernandez be brought to New York, tried, and then given the death penalty. On March 8, 1949, Michigan state officials gave in to the pressure and signed the extradition order. The Lonely Hearts Killers were now facing the electric chair.

The trial of Martha Beck and Raymond Fernandez opened at the Bronx Supreme Court on June 28, 1949, with huge crowds jostling for a place in the courtroom to hear the twisted tale of deception, sex, fraud, and murder.

On August 18, 1949, after 44 days of testimony, the case went to the jury, who worked through the night before delivering their verdict at 8:30 the next morning. They found Beck and Fernandez guilty of first-degree murder. The following Monday, August 22, Judge Pecora sentenced both of them to die in the electric chair.

The Lonely Hearts Killers continued to attract lurid tabloid headlines during the seventeen months that they remained on death row. Eventually, with their appeals exhausted, they were scheduled to die on March 8, 1951. Fernandez went first, the guards having to carry him to the death chamber in a state of nervous collapse. Martha Beck followed, walking confidently, slumping into the chair and voicing a silent "So long" to prison guards before the switch was thrown.

William Bonin & Vernon Butts

William Bonin did not have the best start in life. Born in January 1947, to parents who were both alcoholics, the boy and his two brothers suffered severe neglect and abuse. His father was a compulsive gambler who once lost the family home to his gambling debts, and William's bingo-obsessed mother often left her children unfed, filthy and unclothed, their wellbeing reliant on the charity of neighbors. When she tired of even these meager attempts at parenting, she passed the boys off to their grandfather, a convicted pedophile.

It was no surprise, then, that the youngster got into trouble with the law. In 1957, aged just 10, William was arrested for stealing license plates and sent to a reformatory. Here he suffered yet more abuse. Beatings and inhumane punishments (like submersion in freezing water) were common, as were knifepoint rapes by other inmates. By his teens, Bonin was back in the dubious care of his mother and had become an abuser himself, preying on neighborhood children and even his own brother.

Bonin graduated high school in 1965 and shortly thereafter joined the U.S. Air Force. He served in Vietnam where he logged 700 hours as an aerial gunner and was awarded a Good Conduct medal. It was only after his honorable discharge, in October 1968, that the military became aware that Bonin had sexually assaulted two fellow soldiers at gunpoint.

Back in the States, Bonin lived for a short while with his mother in Connecticut before moving to California where he soon alerted the attention of the authorities. In 1969, he was arrested for kidnapping and sexually assaulting five youths, aged between 12 and 18, in Los Angeles County. In each of these cases, Bonin picked up the boys in his van, handcuffed them and then forced them to perform oral sex before he sodomized them.

Bonin pled guilty, but rather than receiving jail time, he was sent to Atascadero State Hospital where he was examined by a procession of neurologists, psychiatrists, and psychologists. They found some worrying signs, both physical and psychological - suspected damage to the frontal lobe, evidence of manic depression, and several scars on his head suggesting that he'd suffered serious head trauma in the past. Despite this, Bonin secured his release in May 1974, after doctors declared him, "no longer a danger to others."

Within 16 months, he was in trouble again, this time for the gunpoint rape of a 14-year-old hitchhiker named David McVicker. It earned him 1 to 15 years at the California Men's Facility in San Luis Obispo.

Released in October 1978, Bonin moved to an apartment complex in Downey, southeast Los Angeles County, where he found employment as a truck driver. Soon after, he became acquainted with a 43-year-old neighbor named Everett Fraser and started attending the frequent parties that Fraser threw. It was at one of these parties that Bonin first met 22-year-old Vernon Butts, soon to be his accomplice in a horrific murder spree.

Yet, for now, Bonin was still managing to restrain his murderous urges. Less than a year after his release for the McVicker attack, he found himself in custody again, after sexually assaulting a 17-year-old hitchhiker. Bonin was still on probation at this time, and the crime should have sent him back to prison to complete a 15-year stretch. However, an administrative mix-up allowed him to walk free.

Everett Fraser picked Bonin up from the Orange County Jail. He'd later recall that on the drive home, Bonin told him: "No one's going to testify again. This is never going to happen to me again." Shortly after this conversation, the series of murders by the fiend who the media dubbed "The Freeway Killer," began.

The first murder attributed to Bonin was carried out with the aid of his accomplice Vernon Butts, a low-life drifter with a lengthy rap sheet. On the morning of May 28, 1979, 13-year-old Thomas Glen Lundgren left his parents' home in Reseda to visit a friend. The boy was hitchhiking when Bonin and Butts picked him up. His mutilated corpse was found the next day in Agoura. He'd been emasculated, and an autopsy would reveal that he'd been slashed, stabbed, and bludgeoned before being strangled to death.

Two months later, on August 4, 1979, Bonin and Butts abducted 17-year-old Mark Shelton as he walked to a movie theater near Beach Boulevard, Westminster. Shelton was sodomized with foreign objects, which caused his body to go into shock that proved fatal. His corpse was discarded alongside a freeway in San Bernardino County.

Perhaps disappointed with the premature death of their last victim, Bonin and Butts took another teenager the following day. Seventeen-year-old German student, Markus Grabs, was hitchhiking the Pacific Coast Highway when Bonin and Butts offered him a ride. He was bound and taken to Bonin's home where he was sodomized, beaten and stabbed over 70 times. His nude body was discarded in Malibu Canyon.

The unholy duo waited three weeks before striking again. On August 27, the mutilated corpse of 15-year-old Donald Hyden was discovered in a dumpster near the Ventura Freeway. He had last been seen in Santa Monica the previous day. Hyden had been raped and strangled, and his throat had been cut. An attempt had also been made to castrate him.

On September 9, 1979, Bonin and Butts encountered 17-year-old David Murillo cycling to a movie theater. They lured the teenager into Bonin's van where he was bound, raped, bludgeoned, and strangled before his body was discarded alongside Highway 101. Eight days later, they abducted 18-year-old Robert Wirostek as he cycled to work. His ravaged body was discovered on September 19, beside Interstate 10.

Despite the similarities in these crimes, Orange and Los Angeles County officials continued to deny that they had a serial killer in their midst. And they may have felt vindicated in this belief, as nearly three months passed without another murder. However, by the end of November, the Freeway Killer was back, taking three victims in under a fortnight.

The first of those was an unidentified youth who's savagely beaten corpse was discovered in Kern County. The following day, Bonin abducted and strangled 17-year-old Frank Fox, leaving his body on a stretch of highway five miles east of San Diego. Ten days later, he murdered a 15-year-old Long Beach youth named John Kilpatrick. Kilpatrick was last seen leaving his parents' home on his way to meet up with some friends. His body was found beside a road in a remote area of Rialto.

On New Year's Day, 1980, Bonin brutalized and strangled a 16-year-old Rialto youth named Michael Francis McDonald, dumping his body in San Bernardino County, where it was found two days later.

In the last few murders, Bonin had acted alone. On February 3, 1980, he brought in a new accomplice, another sexual psychopath, named Gregory Matthew Miley. The pair picked up 15-year-old Charles Miranda in West Hollywood then drove him to an isolated spot where Bonin sodomized him. When Miley was unable to sustain an erection to do the same, he became frustrated and raped the teen with a blunt object. Bonin then strangled Miranda using the boy's shirt and a tire iron to form a tourniquet. They dumped the body in an alley, but Bonin immediately announced, "I'm still horny. Let's do another one."

A few hours later, they found 12-year-old James McCabe waiting at a stop for a bus to Disneyland. The boy accepted a ride, but as Miley drove, Bonin forced him into the back where he beat and raped him. Later Bonin strangled the boy by forcing a tire iron down on his throat while Miley jumped repeatedly on the child's chest. James McCabe's naked, battered body was found three days later, alongside a dumpster in the city of Walnut. Miley later said that he and Bonin used the $6 found in the boy's wallet to buy lunch.

There was no stopping Bonin now. He was obsessed with murder, addicted to it. He would later tell a court-appointed psychiatrist that he became excited at the prospect of killing someone. He could barely wait for sundown so he could go cruising to pick up his next victim.

A rapid spree of murders followed. Ronald Gatlin, 18, disappeared from North Hollywood on March 14, 1980. His body was discovered the next day in Duarte, beaten strangled and stabbed with an ice pick. Harry Todd Turner, 14, disappeared from Hollywood on March 20. He was discovered five days later, near the Santa Monica Freeway, his body marked with bites and cigarette burns (Bonin was assisted in this murder by an accomplice named William Pugh). Glen Norman Barker, 14, of Huntington Beach, was sexually assaulted and strangled, his body found March 22, beside the Ortega Highway with another body nearby, that of 15-year-old Russell Duane Rugh, who had disappeared while waiting for a bus to work.

And still, the killings continued. Steven Wood, 16, went missing on his way to school on April 10, 1980. His body was found the next day. The same day, Lawrence Eugene Sharp, 18, of Long Beach, disappeared. His body showed up on May 18, in a trash bin behind a Westminster service station.

On April 29, Bonin and Butts abducted Darin Lee Kendrick, 19, from a Stanton store where he worked. In a particularly brutal murder, even by their standards, Kendrick was forced to swallow hydrochloric acid and an ice pick was forced through his ear causing a fatal wound to the upper cervical spinal cord. His body was found the next morning.

On May 19, Bonin asked Butts to go out with him on another killing. When Butts declined, he went out alone and abducted 14-year-old Sean King from a bus stop in Downey. The boy's raped and strangled body was discarded in Yucaipa.

Not long after this latest murder, Bonin invited a 19-year-old, homeless drifter by the name of James Munro to stay with him. Soon he'd persuaded Munro to accompany him on his next murder run.

Unbeknownst to Bonin, his rampage was about to come to an abrupt end.

On May 29, 1980, William Pugh, who had assisted Bonin in the murder of Harry Todd Turner, was picked up on an auto theft charge. Once in custody, Pugh confided to a counselor that he believed William Bonin to be the "Freeway Killer." The counselor passed this information on to LAPD homicide detective John St. John who did a background check on Bonin and picked up his string of convictions for sexually assaulting teenage boys. St. John then arranged for Bonin to be put under surveillance, which began on June 2.

Unfortunately, the surveillance began too late to save Bonin's next victim. On the morning of June 2, 1980, Bonin and James Munro picked up 19-year-old Steven Wells. They lured the youth back to Bonin's apartment and after Bonin and Wells had sex, Bonin offered $200 if Wells would allow himself to be tied up. Wells agreed, but as soon as he was bound, Bonin began assaulting him. According to Munro he went into another room and watched TV, although Bonin disputes this and says Munro participated in the murder.

Once Wells was dead, Bonin and Munro loaded his body into the van and drove to Vernon Butts' apartment. Bonin asked for Butts' advice in disposing of the body and was told, "Try a gas station - like where we dumped the last one."

By June 11, Bonin had been under surveillance for nine days, with no sign of criminality on his part. However, on that day, Bonin went cruising again. The surveillance team watched him try to pick up five separate teenagers before he succeeded in luring a youth into his van. The police followed him as he drove to a deserted parking lot. By the time they approached the van and threw the doors open, Bonin had the boy bound and was in the process of sodomizing him. The Freeway Killer was caught at last.

Once in custody, Bonin confessed to 21 murders, naming Vernon Butts as his primary accomplice and describing each crime in horrifying detail. Butts was arrested on July 25, and the arrests of James Munro and Gregory Miley followed soon after. Police also learned that William Pugh, who'd led them to Bonin, was far from innocent himself, and had participated in the murder of Harry Todd Turner.

Bonin's trial began on November 5, 1981, and lasted until January 5, 1982. The jury deliberated for six days before delivering a guilty verdict in 10 of the murders and recommending the death penalty.

However, it would be 14 years before that sentence was eventually carried out. On February 23, 1996, William Bonin became the first person to be executed by lethal injection in the state of California.

Of Bonin's accomplices, Vernon Butts committed suicide in custody three months after his arrest. Miley, Munro, and Pugh all agreed to testify against Bonin to avoid the death penalty. Miley and Munro received life terms. Pugh got six years on a reduced charge of manslaughter.

John Bunting & Robert Wagner

John Bunting was born on September 4, 1966, in Inala, a suburb of Brisbane, Australia. His early childhood was by all accounts normal until, at age 8, he was sexually assaulted by a friend's older brother. After that, he became moody and insular. He also began indulging in at least one practice that is common among fledgling serial killers. He started hurting animals. A favorite pastime was to drop insects and other small creatures into a vat of acid.

By his teens, the undersized, near-sighted, and somewhat pudgy Bunting had discovered a new outlet for his anger. He became a neo-Nazi, buying completely into the warped ideology of that movement and developing a deep loathing of gays, pedophiles, drug addicts, and other "wasters" in society. That hatred would follow him into adulthood, as would his enjoyment of inflicting pain on living creatures. At 22, he was working in an abattoir, and bragging to his friends about the pleasure he derived from slaughtering animals. Worryingly, he'd also begun accumulating a

collection of weapons. By the time he moved to Adelaide, South
Australia in 1991, Bunting was a ticking bomb, primed to explode.

John Bunting, like most of his ilk, was a nobody, a sorry little man
with an ego way disproportionate to his meager achievements in
life. But he did possess one undoubted skill. Like most
psychopaths, he could be extremely persuasive. Before long, he
was poisoning his new neighbors in the Adelaide suburb of
Salisbury North with his hate-filled outpourings. One of those who
paid attention was the hulking and powerfully built, Robert
Wagner.

On the face of it, Wagner made an unlikely convert to Bunting's
ideology. At the time they met, he was living with an openly gay
man named Barry Lane. Still, Wagner's involvement in the series
that would become known as the 'Snowtown Murders,' lay in the
future. Before then, Bunting would commit at least one murder on
his own. The victim was another of his new friends, 22-year-old
Clinton Trezise.

Tresize's 'crime' was that Bunting suspected him of being a
pedophile. Where exactly this suspicion arose from, is unknown,
but Bunting seems to have acted upon the flimsiest of evidence. In
August 1992, he lured Trezise to his home on the pretext of a
social visit. There, he immediately launched into one of his tirades,
accusing Trezise of sexually molesting children. Trezise's
protestations of innocence fell on deaf ears. Snatching up a shovel,
Bunting bludgeoned him to death. He then buried the body in a
shallow grave at Lower Light, South Australia, where it would
remain undiscovered for the next two years.

Clinton Trezise's sudden disappearance caused some consternation but with no evidence to go on, the police investigation soon fizzled out. Bunting, who knew exactly where the missing man was, was hardly going to speak out. He'd spend the next three years wallowing in the 'perfect murder' he'd committed and spewing hate-filled soliloquies. By the time he was ready to kill again, his new friend Robert Wagner was a willing accomplice. The target of their deadly attention was a mentally disabled man named Ray Davies.

Davies lived in a caravan on the property of Bunting's friend, Suzanne Allen. Allen had two young grandsons, and when she confided in Bunting her suspicion that Davis had propositioned the boys, Bunting was beside himself with anger. He promised to 'take care of' the problem. A short while later, in December 1995, Bunting and Wagner paid Davis a visit. He was never seen alive again.

Bunting liked to portray himself as a crusader against child abuse, but he was not averse to profiting from his crimes. Two months after Davies' death, he arrived at Suzanne Allen's house with a tow truck and removed the caravan Davies had been living in, which he later sold. He also started cashing Davies' monthly welfare checks and would continue to do so until his eventual arrest.

The next person to suddenly disappear from Bunting's circle was Suzanne Allen herself. As someone who knew about the Davies murder, Suzanne was a loose end, one that Bunting and Wagner were determined to trim. Allen disappeared early in 1996. Her dismembered remains would later be discovered wrapped in eleven different plastic bags, in the same grave where Davies lay buried. Bunting would claim at his trial that Suzanne had died of a heart attack. However, he failed to report her death and continued collecting her pension payments.

Bunting had now gotten away with three murders and in the manner of serial killers the world over, he must have felt invincible. With Robert Wagner now in tow, he decided to take his campaign of murder to the next level. First, he drew up a list containing the names of everyone he suspected of being a pedophile. Then he fashioned a schematic, using a blank wall in his home. Bunting called this his "Rock Spider Wall" and it consisted of a collage made of Post-It notes, linked together with different colored yarns. On each of the notes was the name of an intended victim. Bunting's method of choosing his next target usually involved approaching the wall with his eyes closed and his hand outstretched. Whoever's name he touched was as good as dead.

There is nothing to suggest that the next victim, Michael Gardiner, was involved in abusing children. Yet he was openly gay, and that was good enough for Bunting who freely professed his belief that all homosexuals were pedophiles. Gardiner was killed in August 1997, his body stored in a barrel that would later be found in the vault of an abandoned bank in Snowtown. One of his feet had been severed, in order to fit the body into its makeshift coffin.

The next to fall victim to the murderous duo was Barry Lane, Robert Wagner's one-time lover. Lane had, in fact, provided

Bunting with most of the names that appeared on the 'Rock Spider Wall.' But neither that, nor his previous relationship with Wagner, was enough to save him.

In October 1997, Lane made a call to his mother, telling her that he was moving away and wanted nothing more to do with her. The call, in fact, had been made under coercion by Bunting, Wagner, and a third accomplice named Thomas Trevilyan. Lane's dismembered body would eventually be found in the Snowtown bank vault, alongside that of Michael Gardiner. All of the bones in his toes were crushed, suggesting that he'd been tortured prior to his death.

Thomas Trevilyan, accomplice in the Barry Lane killing, was the next victim. Trevilyan suffered from mental problems and following the Lane murder, Bunting had remarked to friends that he was afraid Trevilyan would "go mental," and give them away. Bunting and Wagner eliminated their risk in October 1997, driving Trevilyan into the Adelaide Hills and hanging him from a tree. When Trevilyan's body was found a month later, it was assumed that he had committed suicide.

By now, Bunting was married to a woman named Elizabeth Harvey, whose son, James Vlassakis, looked up to him as a father figure. In 1988, a friend of Vlassakis, Gavin Porter, moved into Bunting's home as a guest. Porter was a heroin addict and Bunting took an instant dislike to him, describing him as a "waste" who "no longer deserved to live." The final straw came when Bunting found a used syringe that Porter had carelessly discarded on a couch. Not long after, Bunting and Wagner strangled Porter as he slept in his car in the driveway of Bunting's house. His body was stored in a barrel at the Snowtown vault.

Troy Youde, a half brother of James Vlassakis, was the next victim. Vlassakis had confided to Bunting that Youde had raped him when he was a child and Bunting, seething with rage, had decided to make him pay for it. In August 1998, Bunting, Wagner, and Vlassakis dragged Youde from his bed and murdered him. Another accomplice, Mark Haydon assisted in the removal of the body to Snowtown.

Haydon also helped with the disposal of the next victim. Frederick Brooks, 18, was Haydon's mentally disabled nephew, and Haydon wanted to get rid of him so that he could gain access to his disability payments. Bunting was only too happy to help. He invited Brooks to his house on September 17, 1998. There, Bunting, Wagner, and Vlassakis brutally tortured the helpless teenager before killing him. He, too, ended up at Snowtown.

Bunting and Wagner's next victim was another mentally disabled man, killed so that Bunting could cash his disability checks. Gary O'Dwyer had suffered severe head trauma in a car accident earlier in his life. He had no immediate family, making him an easy target. O'Dwyer was murdered in his Murray Point home in November 1998. His body, later discovered in the Snowtown vault, showed clear signs of torture.

For his next murder, Bunting turned closer to home. The victim was Elizabeth Haydon, wife of his some-time accomplice, Mark Haydon. Elizabeth went missing from her Adelaide home on November 20, 1998. It was Haydon's failure to report her disappearance that would arouse police suspicions and lead to the eventual break in the Snowtown case.

That break, however, would arrive too late to save Bunting and Wagner's last victim. David Johnson, another half-brother of James Vlassakis, was lured to the Snowtown bank on May 9, 1999, on the pretense of viewing a computer for sale. Once there, he was overpowered by Wagner and then tortured into providing his bank details and PIN number. Wagner and Vlassakis then drove to Port Wakefield and attempted to draw money from Johnson's bank account, leaving Johnson in the custody of Bunting. When they returned, Johnson was dead. Bunting and Wagner later dismembered Johnson's body and added a new perversion to their M.O. They fried strips of their victim's flesh and ate it.

But the net was rapidly closing on Bunting and his depraved apprentices. Police inquiries into Elizabeth Haydon's disappearance led them eventually to the abandoned bank in Snowtown. On May 20, 1999, officers searched the premises and discovered eight bodies, concealed in drums in the vault. Bunting, Wagner, Vlassakis, and Haydon were arrested that same day.

John Bunting went on trial in September 2003, and was found guilty on 11 counts of murder. He was sentenced to 11 consecutive life terms without the possibility of parole. Bunting's main accomplice, Robert Wagner, was sentenced to seven life terms, while James Vlassakis was given four life sentences. It is unlikely that any of them will ever taste freedom again. Mark Haydon agreed to testify against his co-accused and was allowed to plead to a reduced charge of assisting in a murder.

Alton Coleman & Debra Brown

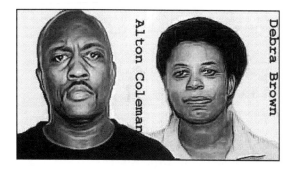

Alton Coleman was born in Waukegan, Illinois on November 6, 1955. His mother was a prostitute who enjoyed having sex with her clients in front of the boy. She later abandoned him to the care of his elderly grandmother. As a child, Alton had the unfortunate habit of wetting his pants, earning him the taunts of his playmates, who called him "Pissy." But that wasn't all that was wrong with Coleman. Law officers who had dealings with him during his teens described him as distant and emotionally stunted. Friends and family recall that he had an overdeveloped sex drive and spent much of his time seeking out new partners, both male, and female.

Coleman's first brush with the law came while he was still a teenager. On that occasion, he was picked up for breaking windows in the Waukegan housing project where he lived. And that was just the first of many arrests. It wasn't long before he had earned a reputation as a troublemaker, even if most of his crimes were petty misdemeanors, usually involving property damage. As anyone who has ever studied serial murder will testify, this is a common characteristic among fledgling serial killers.

And Coleman was soon displaying another trait common to psychopaths – the ability to talk his way out of trouble. He seemed to possess an uncanny knack of convincing jurors that the authorities had the wrong man. Alton's friends had a ready explanation for this. They claimed that he practiced voodoo and relied on supernatural powers to stay one step ahead of the law. The truth was far simpler. Alton Coleman was a skilled liar. And if that didn't work, there was always witness intimidation, something that he employed to beat more than one rap.

Thus, even before the mid-western spree that would propel him to infamy, Alton Coleman's rap sheet was littered with enough arrests to have put him away for several lifetimes, if only prosecutors had been able to make the charges stick. And the crimes were getting more serious. In 1973, he and an accomplice kidnapped, robbed, and raped an elderly woman. That rape charge was dropped after the victim refused to testify and Coleman served just two years for the robbery. Three months after his release, he was found not guilty of another rape, although he did serve time for a lesser charge. Four years later, he was acquitted of yet another sexual assault. A year later, in 1983, an attempted rape charge was dismissed.

1983 was also the year that Coleman met Debra Denise Brown. A mildly retarded girl, due to a head injury suffered in childhood, Brown was engaged to another man at the time. But perhaps she recognized a soul mate in Coleman because she soon ditched her fiancée. Before long she and Coleman were living together.

Not that having a live-in lover in any way blunted Coleman's prodigious sex drive. In July 1983, he was charged with the rape of his 8-year-old niece. That charge was dismissed, but an even more serious one followed a year later when he was indicted for the murder of 9-year-old Vernita Wheat, the daughter of a friend.

Vernita's ravaged body was discovered on May 19, 1984, in an abandoned building four blocks from Coleman's apartment. She had been raped and strangled, and the evidence pointed strongly towards Coleman. Perhaps realizing that he wasn't going to beat the rap this time, he decided to go on the run.

On May 31, 1984, Coleman borrowed a car from his friend Robert Carpenter. He and Brown then hit the road, surfacing five days later in Gary, Indiana. Within weeks of their arrival in that city, two little girls, 9-year-old Annie and her 7-year-old niece, Tamika, disappeared while on their way to a candy store. Annie was found later that day, savagely beaten but still alive. The outcome for Tamika was far worse. Her tiny corpse was found in woodland just outside the city limits. She had been raped and had suffered severe abdominal trauma. It appeared that her killer had stomped on her chest, caving in her ribcage and rupturing all of her vital organs.

As Annie recovered, she revealed the horrendous truth about her ordeal to investigators. She said that she and Tamika had been walking to the store when a man and a woman had approached them. The woman had coaxed them into a car, and they had then been driven to the woods where the couple had begun assaulting them. Tamika suffered the worst of the beating. She had been pinned to the ground by the woman, while the man had kicked and stomped her. Annie had then been forced to have sex with both adults before being beaten some more and left in the woods. Unfortunately, Annie could remember nothing that might help police catch Tamika's killers.

Coleman and Brown, meanwhile, had moved on to new targets. On the day that Tamika's body was discovered, 25-year-old Donna Williams was reported missing by her parents. A week later, Williams' car was found abandoned in Detroit. There was a forged identification card in the glove compartment, with Debra Brown's picture on it. Donna Williams' badly decomposed body would eventually be found in an abandoned house near Wayne State University on July 11. By then, her killers would be the most wanted fugitives in the country.

On June 28, Coleman and Brown were in Dearborn Heights, Michigan where they broke into a house and severely beat an elderly couple before escaping in their car. They showed up next in Toledo, Ohio, where they befriended a woman named Virginia Temple. On July 5, Temple's family, concerned that they hadn't heard from her in a while, called on her home. They found Virginia's children cowering in a darkened room. Searching the home, relatives discovered Virginia's body and that of her 9-year-old daughter, Rachelle, hidden in a crawlspace. Both had been raped and strangled.

The same day that Virginia and Rachelle's bodies were discovered, Coleman and Brown entered the home of Frank and Dorothy Duvendack in Toledo. They bound the couple, ransacked their house, and then escaped in their car, driving it to Dayton, Ohio. On July 12, the deadly duo was in Over-the-Rhine, Ohio, when Tonnie Storey disappeared. Her body was discovered eight days later. She'd been raped and strangled. A bracelet belonging to Virginia Temple was found on the ground beside her.

By now police in Illinois, Wisconsin, Indiana, Ohio, and Michigan were hunting the killers. The federal authorities had also been called in and, on July 12, Alton Coleman was added to the FBI's Ten Most Wanted List as a "special addition," only the 10th person to warrant such attention since the list was initiated in 1950.

But still, the fugitives evaded capture. A day after killing Tonnie Storey they turned up in Norwood, Ohio where they entered the home of Harry and Marlene Waters at 9:30 in the morning. Three hours later they drove away in the Waters' red Plymouth Reliant, leaving Harry Waters with massive skull fractures and his wife, Marlene, dead. The couple was found by their daughter later that day. An autopsy would reveal that Marlene had been struck 25 times, the blows so vicious that they had literally pulped the back of her skull.

On July 17, Coleman and Brown appeared at the home of Reverend Millard Gay and his wife Kathryn, in Williamsburg, Kentucky. The preacher recognized Coleman, having seen his face on TV. When Coleman produced a gun, the reverend asked whether he intended killing them, to which Coleman responded, "I'm not going to kill you, but we generally kill them where we go." Coleman and Brown then tied the couple up and stole their truck. They fled next to Indianapolis where they murdered 75-year-old Eugene Scott, taking his car and continuing on to Evanston, Illinois.

But the net was closing on the fugitives. The police were aware that Coleman had friends in Evanston, and they expected him to show up there sooner or later. On July 20, the pair was spotted sitting on the bleachers in Mason Park. As officers approached, Brown got up and started walking towards an exit, where she was taken into custody. Coleman meanwhile, seemed unperturbed by the presence of the officers. He surrendered without a fight despite having a loaded revolver and a knife in his possession. The hunt was over, now came the complex business of serving justice to the heartless killers.

That would prove to be a mammoth task. A week after Coleman and Brown were arrested, more than 50 law enforcement officials, representing jurisdictions across six states, met to put together a strategy for prosecuting the killers. Michigan was quickly ruled out, as it does not have the death penalty, something that the officials were determined to pursue. It was eventually decided that the first trial would be in Ohio.

Coleman and Brown had committed two murders in the Cincinnati area, the May 1985 slaying of Tonnie Storey, and the murder of Marlene Walters in June 1985. The trials for both of these murders delivered guilty verdicts and death penalties, although, in Brown's case, that was later commuted to life in prison. For Alton Coleman however, there was still the long appeals process, a process that saw his case taken all the way to the U.S. Supreme Court before his death sentence was finally affirmed

Alton Coleman was executed by lethal injection at the Southern Ohio Correctional Facility near Lucasville on Friday, April 26, 2002. There can be few criminals who have so richly deserved that fate.

As for Debra Brown, she remains incarcerated in Ohio. If she were ever to be released, there are a number of death penalty states waiting to put her on trial for her part in the 53-day murder spree.

Loren Herzog & Wesley Shermantine Jr.

Loren Herzog and Wesley Shermantine grew up together on the same street in the small farming community of Linden, California. Virtually inseparable as children the two buddies spent their time doing what other kids do, hanging out, playing ball, and, in their case, exploring the hills, ravines, and mineshafts that surrounded their hometown. Wes' father was a successful contractor, fond of indulging his son with anything his heart desired. An avid hunter and fisherman, Shermantine Sr. would often take the boys with him, teaching them how to cast and how to shoot. It was an idyllic childhood.

But as the boys grew older, troubling signs began to emerge. By high school, they were notorious bullies and troublemakers, heavy drinkers, and eventually, habitual users of hard drugs, particularly methamphetamine (speed). When they moved into an apartment together, their drug taking escalated and they began roaming the highways and bi-ways of San Joaquin County, terrorizing anyone they encountered. They also took to killing people for kicks.

It is impossible to determine when the deadly duo committed their first murder. Investigators who worked their case believe it may have been the killing of Chevelle 'Chevy' Wheeler in 1985.

Chevy was a pretty 16-year-old who attended Franklin High in Stockton, California. On Wednesday, October 16, 1985, she told some of her classmates that she was cutting classes to go with a male acquaintance to Valley Springs. She seemed somewhat uneasy about making the trip and told a friend that, if she didn't return that day, the friend should tell her father where she'd gone. She was last seen getting into a red pickup outside the school.

When Chevy didn't return, the friend, as arranged, informed Mr. Wheeler. He immediately called the police and they soon learned that the man Chevy had agreed to accompany to Valley Springs was Wesley Shermantine. Nineteen-year-old Shermantine was well known to police as a drug user and troublemaker. He also drove a red pickup, like the one Chevy had been seen getting into. Not only that, but Shermantine had called at the Wheeler home on the morning of Chevy's disappearance.

Shermantine was pulled in for questioning and flatly denied any knowledge of her whereabouts or any involvement in her disappearance. Yet, even as he protested his innocence to Chevy's family, detectives sensed that he was lying.

After learning that Shermantine had been staying at a cabin that his family owned in San Andreas, California, the police obtained a search warrant for the premises. There, they found strands of blond hair and blood evidence that was matched to Chevy's type. Unfortunately, it was not enough to bring charges against Shermantine. DNA technology at the time was not sufficiently advanced to make a conclusive match. The evidence went into storage where it would remain for 14 years, before it would come back to haunt Wesley Shermantine.

Over a decade later, on Friday, November 13, 1998, Cyndi Vanderheiden spent the evening with friends at the Linden Inn, a karaoke bar in Linden, California. Also in attendance that night, were Wes Shermantine and his buddy, Loren Herzog. Cyndi was seen speaking to Shermantine during the evening, but nothing came of it. Eventually, she and her friends decided to leave for another bar.

Cyndi had, by now, had quite a lot to drink, so one of her friends insisted on driving her vehicle to their next destination – the Old Corner Saloon in Clements. This particular bar was just a mile from the home Cyndi shared with her parents, so when the group eventually decided to call it a night, Cyndi said she was okay to drive the short distance. Nonetheless, one of her male friends followed her home, to see that she made it okay. The man watched her park in the driveway at approximately 2:30 a.m., but did not wait around until she went into the house. Cyndi's mother would later tell investigators that she heard her daughter pull into the drive, but then dozed off again and didn't heard her actually enter the residence.

The following morning, Cyndi's parents woke to find that she wasn't in the house. Her bed had not been slept in, and her car wasn't in the garage or the driveway. Concerned, Cyndi's father began driving around the neighborhood, hoping to spot his daughter or her vehicle. He found the car parked outside Glenview Cemetery, unlocked, and with Cyndi's purse and cell phone inside. A quick search of the grounds proved that Cyndi wasn't there. Mr. Vanderheiden then drove to the nearest police station.

But a police search proved no more successful at locating the missing girl than her father's had been. Detectives speculated that Cyndi had parked in her parent's driveway for a short while and then, rather than going into the house, she'd driven to the cemetery. But for what purpose? And where was she now? Those questions appeared to have no answers. And they might have remained a mystery had officers working an apparently unrelated cold case not submitted their evidence for reanalysis.

Chevy Wheeler had by now been missing for 13 years. But police in San Joaquin County had always believed that Wesley Shermantine knew a lot more about her disappearance than he was telling. Shermantine had been their prime suspect back in 1985, but investigators had lacked the evidence to charge him. A decade on, and there had been significant advances in DNA technology. The blood and hair samples gathered from Shermantine's cabin were therefore sent to the crime lab again. This time, there was a match. The samples belonged to Chevy Wheeler.

Wes Shermantine was taken into custody on March 18, 1999. But if the police thought that he was going to roll over in the face of their forensic evidence they were wrong. He offered an alternative suspect – his long-time buddy, Loren Herzog. Loren had a key to the cabin, he said, and he'd always had a thing for Chevy. It was he who'd taken her to Valley Springs, he who had killed her.

But Herzog flatly denied the allegations, telling investigators that Shermantine had killed Chevy and had even bragged to him about it. And then, Herzog dropped a bombshell. Not only had Wes killed Chevy Wheeler, he said, he'd also murdered Cyndi Vanderheiden. And, hinted Herzog, there were other murders, too.

The officers were not entirely surprised to hear Shermantine's name mentioned in connection with the Vanderheiden murder. But they were less convinced by Herzog's assertion that he had no involvement in the crime. After all, the two were inseparable, and Herzog's bad reputation was at least the equal of Shermantine's. They began leaning on Herzog, subjecting him to 17 hours of intense interrogation. Eventually, a story began to emerge, one that marked the suspects out as the most ruthless killers in the county's long history.

According to Herzog, Shermantine was responsible for at least five unsolved murders in Northern California, and one in Utah. He (Herzog) had witnessed all of the killings but hadn't actively participated in any of them.

The first murder happened in 1984, he said. He and Wes had been

driving along Highway 88 in the area of Hope Valley, when they'd
spotted a vehicle parked on the side of the road. Shermantine had
pulled over and got out of his truck carrying a shotgun. He'd
approached the vehicle where the driver sat slumped over the
wheel, apparently intoxicated. Then, without provocation or
warning, he'd lifted the shotgun and fired at the driver from close
range, obliterating his skull. A check on police records proved that
just such a murder had occurred. The victim was 41-year-old
Henry Howell, a resident of Santa Clara, California.

Two months later, according to Herzog, he and Wes were again
prowling the highways, this time in the area of Roberts Island,
southwest of Stockton. Spotting a 1982 Pontiac by the roadside,
Shermantine had pulled over. He and Herzog then got out of their
truck, both carrying shotguns. Again, Shermantine had fired
without warning, killing the driver, 35-year-old Howard King, as
he sat behind the wheel. The pair had then dragged the passenger,
Paul Cavanaugh, 31, from the vehicle. Shermantine had shot him as
he begged for his life.

This double homicide was again verified by police records. In fact,
eyewitnesses had reported seeing a red pickup, similar to the one
Shermantine drove, in the area. Tire impressions taken at the
scene would later be matched to Shermantine's truck.

In September of the following year, Herzog and Shermantine met
24-year-old Robin Armtrout at a park in Stockton and convinced
her to go for a drink with them. Instead, they drove her to a field
outside Linden where, according to Herzog, Shermantine beat and
raped the young woman before stabbing her to death. Her nude

body was later found by a hunter. A witness had seen her getting into a red pickup with two men.

Of the Cyndi Vanderheiden murder, Herzog said that he and Shermantine had arranged to meet Cyndi at the Glenview Cemetery under the pretense of doing some drugs. The three had met up at the graveyard, leaving Cyndi's car there while they drove back to Linden in Shermantine's pickup. While they were driving, Shermantine pulled a knife and ordered Cyndi to perform oral sex on him. He then stopped the truck and raped Cyndi, before slashing her throat. Cyndi's blood would later be found on the passenger-side headrest of Shermantine's car.

Herzog also implicated Shermantine in the 1994 shooting of a hunter in northern Utah. Police there confirmed that the murder had occurred and was still unsolved.

So far, detectives had heard Loren Herzog's side of the story, recording it all on videotape. Now, they played that tape to Shermantine who unsurprisingly denied his involvement and insisted that Herzog was the killer and that he (Shermantine) had been the hapless bystander.

As the former friends continued to trade accusations, the police were left to wonder which one, if either, was telling the truth. One thing did bother investigators, though. According to both Herzog and Shermantine's statements, they'd killed five people before they'd even turned 21. Then they'd committed no more murders for over a decade. That just didn't ring true, especially as Shermantine was often heard to boast that he'd "disappeared" 19 people. On one notable occasion, he'd apparently pushed a woman's head to the ground during a confrontation and told her: "Listen to the heartbeats of the people I've buried here. Listen to the heartbeats of the families I've killed."

Wesley Shermantine Jr. went on trial in November 2000, in Santa Clara. Despite his continued protestations of innocence, he was found guilty of the murders of Chevy Wheeler, Cyndi Vanderheiden, Paul Cavanaugh, and Howard King. He was sentenced to death and currently awaits execution at San Quentin. In the years since his incarceration, he has offered to point out the location of various bodies in exchange for cash. His offers have always been declined.

Loren Herzog's trial, for the murders of Cyndi Vanderheiden, Howard King, Paul Cavanaugh, Robin Armtrout, and Henry Howell, took place in August 2001 He was found not guilty of killing Armtrout and Howell, but guilty of the first-degree murders of Vanderheiden, King, and Cavanaugh. The sentence of the court was 78 years in prison. However, these convictions were overturned in August 2004, after it was found that police had improperly interrogated him.

Over the protests of local residents and politicians, Loren Herzog was freed under strict parole conditions in July 2010. Just over 18 months later, on January 16, 2012, he was found dead in his trailer. Herzog had hung himself, leaving behind a suicide note that read, "Tell my family I love them."

A month after Herzog's death, Shermantine provided maps to five burial sites which he claimed were Herzog's "boneyards." Here police found the remains of Cyndi Vanderheiden and Chevelle Wheeler. There were also over 1,000 bone fragments from unknown victims.

Fred and Rosemary West

Throughout the spring and summer of 1994, the world's media flocked to the historic city of Gloucester, in the southwest of England. Their interest was focused particularly on an ordinary three-story house at 25 Cromwell Street. If the stories emanating from this address were to be believed, then it had been the venue for one of the most wanton chapters in British criminal history, a sordid saga of sexual perversion, torture, incest, murder, and dismemberment.

It all began on February 24, 1994. On that ordinary Thursday afternoon, police officers descended on the home of a man named Frederick West. Fred was not there when the police arrived, but the door was opened by his sullen, heavy-set wife. The officers explained to Mrs. West why they were there. After that, she immediately placed a call to her husband, who was working at a house some 20 minutes drive away.

"You'd better get back home," she told Fred. "They're going to dig up the garden, looking for Heather."

Frederick Walter Stephen West was born on September 29, 1941, in the Herefordshire village of Much Marcle. His parents, Walter and Daisy, were farm laborers who, despite their precarious financial situation, had seven children, all of them born within a ten-year-period. Walter West was a strict disciplinarian who (according to Fred) routinely committed incest with his daughters. "I made you, so I'm entitled to have you," was an oft-spoken credo.

Fred got on well with his father, but his relationship with his mother was even closer. He was her favorite, and she doted on the boy, often appearing at Fred's school to harangue teachers who disciplined him. These interventions, however, could do nothing to help Fred academically. He was hardly the brightest star in the galaxy. By the time he dropped out of school at age 15, he was functionally illiterate, barely able to write his own name. Thereafter, he took the only employment available to him. He became a farm laborer, like his parents.

And yet Fred appears to have accepted his lot with a kind of good-natured pragmatism. He had two interests in life, his motorcycle, and chasing after girls. With his somewhat simian looks, coarse hair, and gap-toothed smile, he was hardly the lothario he hoped to be. Yet despite his scruffy appearance and poor personal hygiene, some girls were attracted to him. As for the others, he pursued them regardless and was unfazed by rejection.

When Fred was 17, his other obsession in life brought him to grief. He was involved in a motorcycle accident that left him in a coma for a week. As a result of his injuries, a metal plate had to be inserted into his head, while severe leg fractures left one appendage permanently shorter than the other. And the accident had another side effect. It made him prone to sudden fits of rage.

Nonetheless, Fred was back on his feet sooner than expected. After recovering from the accident, he met a pretty 16-year-old named Catherine Bernadette Costello, known to all as Rena. Costello was an accomplished thief and a habitual liar. She and Fred hit it off immediately and were soon lovers. When she announced that she was returning to Scotland, Fred descended into a funk that lasted all of two days. Thereafter, he resumed his none-too-subtle pursuit of women. On one occasion, he stuck his hand up a woman's skirt, and she responded by lashing out at him, causing him to fall down a fire escape and strike his head. It has been speculated that this fall, along with the motorcycle accident, resulted in permanent brain damage.

By 1961, the 20-year-old Fred had already accumulated a lengthy police record. The first entry on that docket was for the theft of cigarette cases from a jewelry store. That earned him a fine. Then there was the theft of materials from the building site where he worked. He was acquitted on that charge but it cost him his job. Then he stood accused of impregnating a 13-year-old girl, the granddaughter of one of his father's friends. Again, he walked free, after his attorney entered a plea of diminished responsibility due to the head injuries he'd suffered. He'd hardly learned his lesson, though. He continued to pursue underage girls and to pilfer anything he could get his hands on, regardless of value. His response, when challenged about his activities, was always the same: "Everyone does it."

In the summer of 1962, Fred's old girlfriend, Rena Costello, returned from Scotland, and the two immediately took up where they'd left off. They appeared perfectly matched. Rena was only 17 but already she had a police record for prostitution and burglary. She was also pregnant, the result of a dalliance with a Pakistani bus driver.

None of this seemed to bother Fred. In fact, he seemed overjoyed at the pregnancy, telling everyone who would listen that the child was his. In November 1962, he moved with Rena to Scotland, where they soon married. Rena's daughter, Charmaine, was born in March 1963. Thereafter, Fred concocted a ridiculous story to account for Charmaine's ethnicity. He told his mother that Rena's baby had been stillborn and that he and Rena had thereafter adopted a mixed-race child. The West family appears to have believed him.

Meanwhile, Fred had gotten a job driving an ice cream truck, something that suited him down to the ground. His easy line of chatter coupled with his apparent politeness and sincerity allowed him to seduce a number of the teenaged girls who flocked to his vehicle to buy ice cream.

In 1964, Rena was pregnant again, eventually bearing Fred a daughter, who they named Anna Marie. But in the midst of this joyous event, disaster struck. Fred was involved in an accident with his ice cream van that resulted in the death of a four-year-old boy. Although he was cleared of any blame, he decided to return with his family to Gloucester. Rena's friend, Ann McFall, went with them, but it wasn't long before Rena was homesick and agitating for a move back to Scotland. When Fred refused, she left on her own, abandoning her children. When she returned in July 1966, she found Fred and Ann McFall living together with Charmaine and Anna Marie in a trailer. Apparently unperturbed by the living arrangements, Rena also moved in.

Fred was, by now, working at a slaughterhouse, something that certain commentators believe had a profound effect on his psyche. Whether that is true or not, we do know that around the time of Rena's return, there were a number of sexual assaults in and around Gloucester, committed by a man who closely matched Fred West's description. Yet, despite West's history as a sex offender, he was never questioned by police.

Then, in early 1967, Ann McFall disappeared. Ann had become pregnant by Fred and had been pressuring him to divorce Rena and marry her. Her whereabouts would remain a mystery for nearly three decades, until Fred West led investigators to her burial site in nearby woods. A forensic examination of the remains would reveal that the fingers and toes had been removed, a signature that West would repeat during his later crimes.

That, however, lay in the future. For now, Fred sent Rena out to work as a prostitute while he stayed home to look after the children. He also started sexually molesting his 5-year-old stepdaughter, Charmaine.

In January 1968, a pretty 15-year-old named Mary Bastholm was abducted from a bus stop in Gloucester. Fred West was never charged with the crime, but there are a number of reasons to believe that he was the man responsible. Mary worked at the Pop-In Café, which Fred frequented. She'd been on friendly terms with Fred's former lover, Ann McFall, and had also, according to a witness, been seen inside Fred's car. Given the sexual assaults on other young women in the area, it is not a stretch to imagine that Fred might have been responsible for Mary's disappearance.

In February 1968, Fred's mother, Daisy, died from complications caused by a gallbladder operation. Fred had been close to his mother, and her death hit him hard. Shortly after, Rena absconded again, leaving Fred to care for the children on his own. But Daisy and Rena would be supplanted in Fred's affections before the year was out. In November 1968, he met the woman who would become his partner in love and in crime, a 15-year-old named Rosemary Letts.

Rosemary Letts was born on November 29, 1953, in Devon, England. The Letts family was plagued by mental problems. Rose's mother, Daisy, suffered from chronic depression. Her father, Bill, was a diagnosed schizophrenic, a violent, abusive man, not averse to using his fists on his wife and children. He is also believed to have sexually abused his daughters.

As if this wasn't enough, Rose had another strike against her. While pregnant, Daisy had undergone electroshock therapy to deal with her depression, and this appears to have caused harm to her unborn daughter. As a baby, Rose would rock herself obsessively in her cot, a habit she carried into childhood when she'd sit nodding her head for hours on end. It also became clear early on that she was a bit "slow." At school, they called her, "Dozy Rosie," reflecting her inability to grasp even simple concepts. What she lacked in intelligence, though, she made up for in guile. She was particularly manipulative when it came to her father. She was his favorite and thus escaped the savage beatings meted out to her siblings.

By her teens, Rose was a pretty girl, with big, dark eyes, and long brown hair. She had also developed a vicious temper and a sexual precociousness that belied her tender years. Barely 15, she already had a string of lovers, all of them older, married men. There were also well-founded rumors that she was involved in a sexual relationship with her father.

Thus, in 1968, Rose Letts' life was going nowhere. She was uneducated, bad-tempered, and not very quick-witted. Her primary interest seemed to be seducing older men, who were happy enough TO share her bed but disinclined to stick around. Had Rose continued on that trajectory, it is doubtful that we would ever have heard of her. But then she met Frederick West.

It is easy to see what might have drawn the pair together. Neither

was very bright, and they were both obsessed with sex. At 27, Fred
was nearly twice Rosemary's age, but that would have been of
little concern to her; at 15, she was comfortably within the age
group that he typically targeted.

Bill Letts, perhaps seeing Fred as a rival for Rose's affections, was
dead-set against the relationship. When he found out that Rose
was sleeping with Fred, he first reported the matter to Social
Services and then threatened to beat Fred up. Neither of these
measures was effective in separating the pair. When Rose did
eventually go back to live with her father, it was because Fred had
been sent to prison for various petty thefts. By then, she was
already pregnant with his child.

After Fred was released, Rose went to live in his trailer and
became a de facto stepmother to Charmaine and Anna Marie. In
1970, she gave birth to a daughter, who she and Fred named
Heather.

Three young children would be a handful for any mother, let alone
a 16-year-old with anger management issues. Neither was Fred
much help. He was in and out of prison, and when he was home, he
was unable to find work. Making ends meet was a constant
struggle, leaving Rose in a perpetual bad mood. She took her
frustrations out on the children, especially Rena's offspring,
Charmaine and Anna Marie.

In the summer of 1971, Fred returned from his latest term of incarceration to find Charmaine gone. Rose said that Rena had come to get her, but the truth was more sinister than that. Charmaine's body would be recovered some 20 years later, buried under the kitchen floor at Midland Road where the Wests had lived before moving to Cromwell Street. The fingers, toes, and kneecaps of the corpse had been removed, a signature of Fred West's later crimes. It can therefore be assumed that Rose eventually broke down and admitted to Fred that she'd killed Charmaine, and that he had then buried the body.

But Charmaine's death had created a problem for Fred. In August 1971, Rena showed up and demanded to know where her daughter was. Fred told her that Charmaine was staying with friends and would be home the next day. That night he got her drunk and then strangled her. Rena's body was dismembered and then buried in a field, close to her old friend Ann McFall.

In January 1972, Fred and Rose made their relationship official when they tied the knot at the Registry Office in Gloucester. In July of that year, Rose gave birth to another daughter, Mae, and the West family moved to a new home, a rundown terrace at number 25 Cromwell Street. Fred seemed particularly pleased that the house had a cellar. He once told a neighbor (only half-jokingly) that he was planning to turn it into a torture chamber. Not long after, he committed his first atrocity down there, raping his eight-year-old daughter, Anna Marie, while Rose held her down.

And Fred West's perversions were not restricted to incest and pedophilia. At around this time, he started running ads in 'swinger' magazines, inviting men of West Indian extraction to sleep with his wife. Soon Rose was running a thriving prostitution business out of their home. But Fred hadn't done it just for the money. He was a voyeur, who enjoyed watching the action through a peephole.

In late 1972, Fred and Rose hired a pretty 17-year-old named Caroline Roberts as a nanny. Caroline was good at the job and fond of the West children, but she soon quit after both of the Wests made sexual advances towards her. On December 6, 1972, Fred and Rose were driving around Gloucester when they spotted Caroline at a bus stop. They offered her a lift and then convinced her to go home with them by telling her how much the children missed her. Once there, Caroline was overpowered and stripped naked. She was then brutally raped by Fred and sexually assaulted by Rosemary. Fred then warned her not to tell anyone. "I'll keep you in the cellar and let my black friends have you," he threatened. "And when they're finished I'll kill you and bury you under the paving stones."

Caroline Roberts was so traumatized by her ordeal, so terrified by Fred's threats, that she resolved to say nothing. But the violent assault had left her in pain and with severe bruising to her body. When Caroline's mother saw the injuries, she convinced her daughter to go to the police and both Fred and Rose were arrested. A hearing was scheduled for January 1973, but Fred was able to convince the magistrate that Caroline had been a willing participant. The charge was reduced to indecent assault, and the Wests walked away with a paltry fine.

Still, Caroline was lucky, the next woman to stay at 25 Cromwell

Street would not get out alive. Lynda Gough was a seamstress who moved in to help care for the children and disappeared around April 1973. She would later be found buried under the garage.

The Wests had, by now, acquired a taste for murder. In November that year, they abducted 15-year-old Carol Ann Cooper as she walked home from the cinema. The girl was held as a plaything for the sexually depraved couple, then snuffed out when she'd outlived her entertainment value. Her remains were added to the growing boneyard underneath 25 Cromwell Street.

A little over a month later, on December 27, university student Lucy Partington went missing after visiting a friend. Lucy left to catch a bus at around 10 p.m. and was never seen alive again. Like Carol Ann Cooper, she'd been abducted by the Wests and taken back to Cromwell Street. There, she was sexually tortured for several days, then murdered, dismembered, and interred in a shallow grave. (A week after Lucy vanished, Fred West went to a hospital with a serious cut to his hand. Investigators would later speculate that he had cut himself while dismembering her corpse.)

Lucy Partington and Carol Ann Cooper were, of course, reported missing by their families. But there was nothing to connect either of the girls to Fred and Rose. Over the next year, three more women – Therese Siegenthaler, 21, Shirley Hubbard, 15, and Juanita Mott, 18, – were raped, tortured, and killed by the Wests, their dismembered remains buried under the cellar floor at 25 Cromwell Street. When found, their corpses bore witness to the suffering and indignity they'd been subjected to. Shirley's head had been wrapped entirely in duct tape with a plastic tube inserted into her nose so that she could breathe; Juanita was trussed in such a way that it appeared she'd been suspended from the beams on the cellar ceiling.

In 1977, Fred carried out construction work at 25 Cromwell Street, dividing the upper floor into a warren of tiny rooms so that the Wests could take in lodgers. One of those who moved in was an 18-year-old former prostitute named Shirley Robinson, who became involved in sexual relationships with both Fred and Rose and eventually became pregnant by Fred. At the same time, Rose was pregnant by one of her West Indian clients. But while Fred seemed delighted at the idea of his wife carrying another man's child, Rose was less thrilled by Shirley's pregnancy. Matters came to a head when Shirley foolishly tried to displace Rose in Fred's affections. She was killed in May 1978 and buried in the back garden along with her unborn baby.

Rose gave birth to two more children in 1978, a mixed-race daughter named Tara and another girl, fathered by Fred, who they named Louise. But those were not the only pregnancies at Cromwell Street. Fred had by now been sexually abusing Anna Marie for six years and inevitably the 14-year-old fell pregnant. Perhaps thankfully, the pregnancy was ectopic and had to be terminated. Anna Marie would eventually escape her father's clutches by leaving home in 1980. By then, Fred and Rose had committed another murder, that of teenager Alison Chambers. Alison ended up buried in the garden beside Shirley Robinson

Over the next three years, Rosemary kept up her seemingly perpetual cycle of pregnancies. Barry was born in June 1980,

Rosemary Junior (another mixed-race child) in April 1982, Lucyanna in July 1983. Fred continued to sexually abuse his daughters Heather and Mae, threatening them with dire consequence if they told anybody.

That wall of silence held until 1986, when Heather confided in a friend, who repeated the story to her parents. Unfortunately, the parents were friends of the Wests and Fred soon got to hear of Heather's indiscretion. Heather disappeared soon after.

Fred and Rose explained their daughter's disappearance by saying that Heather had run away with a lesbian lover. To their children, however, they told a different story. Misbehavior was greeted with the threat that they would "end up under the patio like Heather."

It is not known whether the West's committed any more murders after the death of Heather. If they did, those bodies were disposed of somewhere other than 25 Cromwell Street. What is certain, though, is that Fred continued raping his daughters. In July 1992, one of the girls told a friend, who told her mother, who reported the matter to the police.

The investigation was assigned to Detective Constable Hazel Savage, who was well acquainted with Fred West's many crimes and misdemeanors. On August 6, Detective Savage arrived at 25 Cromwell Street with a search warrant. As a result of that search, Fred was arrested for the rape and sodomy of a minor, while Rose was arrested for assisting in the rape. Hazel Savage then started questioning the West children and learned for the first time of the disappearances of Charmaine, Rena, and Heather, and of the oft-repeated threat of joining Heather under the patio.

The investigation into the Wests' nefarious deeds, however, was anything but simple. After their initial statements, the children clammed up, leaving the rape case against Fred in jeopardy. It seemed that Fred and Rose would walk away scot-free. And they might well have done so, but for the persistence of Hazel Savage.

Savage had launched a countrywide search for Heather West and turned up nothing, not a tax return, not a bank account, no evidence of a doctor's visit. Heather, it appeared, had fallen off the face of the earth and that, to Savage, meant one of two things. Either Heather had left the country or she was dead. Detective Savage was beginning to favor the latter. After questioning the West children again, she began to fear that perhaps the rumors were true after all. Perhaps Heather really was buried under the patio.

On February 24, 1994, a forensic team arrived at 25 Cromwell Street to carry out a search. It was while evacuating the garden on day two that the first human remains were discovered. Fred and Rosemary West's deadly secrets, so fiercely protected for over two decades, were about to be dragged out into the light.

Fred West was taken into custody on February 25. Under interrogation, he quickly admitted that the remains were those of his daughter, Heather, and confessed to killing her. He'd later withdraw that confession but as more and more skeletal remains were recovered from the garden and cellar, he eventually broke down admitted to ten murders, including that of his first wife, Rena. Rose, he insisted wasn't involved.

But despite Fred's continued insistence that he had acted alone, the evidence against Rose continued to build and in April 1994 she was arrested and charged with ten counts of murder. Fred would eventually be charged with 12 murders, but he'd never stand trial. He hanged himself in his cell at Winson Green Prison, Birmingham on January 1, 1995.

Rosemary West went on trial at Winchester Crown Court in 1995 and was found guilty on each of ten counts of murder. She was sentenced to life imprisonment with the recommendation that she should never be released. That decision was later ratified by the Home Secretary, meaning Rosemary West will die in prison.

For more True Crime books by Robert Keller please visit

http://bit.ly/kellerbooks

52543565R00090

Made in the USA
Lexington, KY
16 September 2019